BROKEN COMPASS

MICHAEL TAYLOR

Michael Taylor

Broken Compass
Copyright © Michael Taylor
First published 2019
ISBN: 978-0-6485089-1-5
All rights reserved. Without limiting the rights under copyright reserved above, no part of this publication may be reproduced, stored in or introduced into a database and retrieval system or transmitted in any form or any means (electronic, mechanical, photocopying, recording or otherwise) without the prior written permission of both the owner of copyright and the above publisher.

FACEBOOK
https://www.facebook.com/brokencompass2019/

Published with the assistance of https://angelkey.com.au
Cover Design by Ian Lewis @ Angel Key Publications P/L

Contents

Summary IV
The Beginning 1
Nan and Pops 6
Meeting Eddie's Family 7
Horses 10
First Crime 14
George's 18
Boys Home 25
Move to Footscray 31
Wolfman 35
Stealing Cars 41
Romper Stomping 46
Meeting Sam 53
The Crew 58
Tins of Heroin 68
Boggo Road 83
Meeting Deb 91
Uncle Rob 106
Gay Encounter 116
Close To Death 122
Living On An Island 138
Gypsie 152
Heading South 159
Getting To Know Trinette 163
Making It Work 166
Family 169
Money Trouble 177
Life Goes On 182

Summary

'Broken Compass' is a story based on actual events. The storyline involves episodes of chilling crime, gangs and drugs.

'Broken Compass' is centred on facts and events surrounding the highs and lows of what life can be like growing up on the streets.

Crime, gangs and drugs unfold through the pages as you read through 'Broken Compass'.

A real-life story of struggle and survival while growing up, followed by a strong determination to find peace and serenity in prime years.

But, there is a turning point!

The turning point for me was: The realisation that it is up to me, and me only, to make my own life-changing decision. Ultimately, by changing my life direction.

Pointing your compass in the right direction may be the starting point to a new beginning.

It was for me!

Watch my Facebook page here:
https://www.facebook.com/brokencompass2019/

Chapter 1

THE BEGINNING

I was born in Footscray Hospital, Melbourne, Victoria, in 1963. It was a working-class industrial suburb with dockyards, a transport company, a meatworks and factories; a very old area of Melbourne.

My mother, Alice, was sixteen years old when she met my father. By the time she had given birth to me, her first child, she was only nineteen years old. Twelve months later, to the day, mum gave birth to my brother, Mark. Within a few months, mum was pregnant again with her third child, a girl, Veronica.

My father Jim was a selfish man who gambled, went out with his mates and stole items from warehouses and other places to make money. He would come home whenever he felt like it. He would act abusively to mum.

Around the time mum was pregnant with my sister Veronica, she decided to leave my dad because she was not happy in the relationship. She found herself a bungalow in Sunshine, a suburb of Melbourne, and we made our home there.

Back in those times, you didn't receive any help from the government if you were struggling financially. There were no payments for single mums. You had to ask your family for assistance. However, my mum couldn't do this, as her mother was quite strict in her beliefs in regards to loaning or assisting anyone where money was concerned. Mum came from a large family of six brothers and six sisters.

At this time, none of my mother's family could afford to help her. Mum's family were too young, or they were setting up with their own lives financially and not in a position to help. So, mum was on her own. Mum landed herself a job in a supermarket, packing shelves, while Mark and I were being looked after by a neighbour.

Welfare officers came to our home when my younger brother Mark was about four months old. They said they were going to take Mark away from mum because they didn't think she was coping. My brother, Mark, was removed from our home and put into an orphanage.

Around six months later, a family from England adopted him and took him back to their home in England to raise him. Mum never saw Mark again until he was forty years old. I will explain more about this later.

However, mum knew that she still had me to look after, and was about to have another child. She continued working until she was about eight months pregnant with Veronica when she had to give up her job. Unable to pay the rent and with nowhere to go, we were out on the street. She sat with me and a suitcase on the kerbside crying, not knowing what to do next.

While sitting there, a car came along, slowed down and stopped. It was Merv who used to work with mum at the supermarket. He would often talk with mum during their lunch breaks at work, and they got along pretty well. He saw that mum looked upset and had stopped to see if she was alright.

The Beginning

"Hi Alice, are you ok? I saw you sitting at the kerb with your hands up to your face crying. I wanted to see what was wrong, and see if I could help," Merv said.

Mum explained her problem to Merv. "Well, you can come to stay at my place. I have a spare room. I know you can't pay rent for the room, but if you like, you can do some housekeeping and cook my meals. I'm hopeless at it, and you would be doing me a favour," he said.

Mum thought his offer was wonderful, and it was nice of him. She knew him from work; it had always been nice to talk to him. Mum felt she would be safe, and it would solve her problems. Mum took up his offer and hopped into his car, feeling better, thinking that things were looking up.

On arriving at Merv's house, we noticed that it was a bit of a mess. Mum started cleaning it up straight away and made Merv some dinner. Mum appeared to have settled in quite well within a short time. Every day she would clean and tend to the washing, it made her feel useful again. When Merv arrived home, she would have his dinner prepared, ready for him.

After a month went by, Mum started to go into labour. Luckily for her, Merv was home this day, so he rushed her to the hospital. Within a few hours, my sister Veronica was born. Mum seemed happy to me. After a couple of days, she went home. On arriving home, we noticed that Merv had been shopping. Merv bought nappies and a second-hand cot. Mum thought how thoughtful and kind of Merv to give her so much help.

Merv came home one night from work excited and told mum that during his lunch break, he sat for his truck license. He was going to look for work driving so that he could earn more money. Mum said to him, "Good on you."

In time I guess Mum and Merv got closer and started having feelings for each other. Soon, she was sleeping in his room. Mum turned the spare room into a room for my newborn sister and me. Mum was thinking about how things had turned around for us and appeared to be feeling much happier.

One morning, about three months later, mum walked into the room I shared with my sister only to find that Veronica was blue and wasn't breathing. Mum telephoned the ambulance. When the ambulance arrived, the paramedics went into the bedroom to find that my sister was dead. They weren't able to revive her; it was terrible.

My mum was screaming and crying. They took my sister away. Later they told mum that it was cot death, or sudden infant death syndrome. Sudden infant death syndrome wasn't a common thing, and not heard of much in those days, and it was very hard for her to cope. Mum felt that things were turning bad again.

Veronica had passed away within three months of her birth.

I believe mum couldn't cope with the death of my sister, Veronica; and that was the beginning of all my mother's troubles in her life. The passing away of Veronica was enough to put mum into a depressive state of mind. She started drinking and gave up on life in some ways.

Later Merv came home from work and heard what had happened. He was in shock and sat with mum for hours feeling numb. Merv continued to work, keeping things going, within a few months, mum was pregnant again. Merv offered to marry mum, and so they did. Months later, my sister Karen came into the world. Things were going along

The Beginning

fine now. Merv got a job driving trucks interstate. Things seemed to be back to normal again.

After a few months mum told Merv "I have some good news," she was pregnant again. Merv was happy with the news, so they had to get a bigger place to live. They found a house in North Melbourne, which was only a few kilometres from Merv's work and closer to the city.

Life was traveling along nicely. Mum went into the hospital and gave birth to a little girl, Leanne. However, in only a few weeks she also died of cot death.

After that, Mum became miserable, and things started to change for her. She began drinking again, and with Merv being away interstate, she was alone with my sister Karen and I. She began to blame herself for the loss of three children, Mark, Veronica and Leanne and became very depressed. She felt that she couldn't ask anyone for help, so she had to deal with things on her own.

Merv would come home from work and notice dirty dishes, washing not done and mum drinking and taking pills. After a while, I guess Merv realised that their relationship had started to deteriorate. Within the next twelve months, they had separated, and mum went to Nan and Pop's place to live.

Chapter 2

NAN AND POPS

Nan was a very hard woman and would often tell Mum that she had ruined two marriages; of course, this made mum feel worse. Maybe Nan thought this way because while Pop was away in the Navy, Nan had to raise all of her children by herself. I supposed Pop would only be home long enough to get Nan pregnant and would go back off to war. I guess raising all those kids alone must have been hard.

While I was growing up at my grandparents' house, Nan would cook apple pies and scones. I would sit at the table with her listening to the races on the radio as we waited for them to cook. Pop would either be watching war movies or be out in his shed building things. Anyhow, we were able to live back at Nan and Pop's, and I loved it there.

Pop would tell me war stories. When I was about four years old; mum would go out all the time and come home drunk. Mum and Nan would fight, but Pop would say to me, "Come with me, leave them to fight and sort things out." Pop was never one to get angry. I guess he had already seen too much fighting at war.

Chapter 3

Meeting Eddie's Family

About a year later, mum started going out dating. One day she came home and told me about this guy she had met. His name was Eddie. She thought I'd like him and get along well. He drove trucks. Eddie had three brothers named Davie, Fred and Joe. Eddie would come to Nan and Pop's every weekend to take us out.

Eddie seemed like a nice man. Often he would take me hunting with him. I would follow him picking up rabbits after he shot them, and we would carry them back to camp, where we would cook up a feed. I loved it. He showed me how to set traps and make a fire.

When I was a bit older, about eight or nine, he said, "Here you go, have a go at shooting cans with a 22 rifle."

It made me feel quite grown up. When I was about eleven years old, I had a go with a shotgun, and it knocked me on my arse. I think that's when I got the taste for guns. I guess it gave me a sense of power.

Eddie had been in Vietnam during the war and was an excellent S.A.S. Soldier. He would never talk about the war though; not like Pop, he loved scaring me with his stories about the Japanese. Eddie loved camping, fishing and working on cars. He was a hardworking man and mum probably saw a lot of good in him.

Mum moved into a house with him, which they had bought together. It was in Williamstown in Melbourne, a very old suburb, a navy dock area, lots of pubs, and a lot of bluestone buildings which the convicts built back in the settlement days. People who lived there were working-class, they worked at the docks or the local meatworks. There were a lot of people who came from England, Germany, and there were Dutch and Italians etc. After the Second World War, many had migrated to this country.

Mum put me into school; I started in grade three. The school was made of bluestone and had a bell tower; it was very English. There was a Catholic school across the road where the students would always get into fights with the students from our school. Things got so bad that they changed the times we had lunch and the times of day when we finished school, so there wouldn't be so many fights.

In those days, if you got into trouble, you would get the strap or cane, depending on which teacher you had. I must have been punished with the strap about six times a week on average. I hated school but enjoyed lunchtime as I would play Australian Rules football, and I would swap my lunch with the Italian and Greek boys. They had different food for lunches, which I had never tasted before.

Mum would give me Vegemite or jam sandwiches. I guess I was getting bored with my lunches, as did the Italian and Greek boys with theirs. They'd never tasted Vegemite before, and they seemed to like it. I liked the lasagne, Spaghetti Bolognese and Greek salads etc.

Now and then mum would give me two dollars to take to school to buy lunch at the tuckshop. In the morning you would write what you wanted on a brown paper bag and put the money inside and leave it at the canteen. I would get a meat pie and a can of coke. It was a treat, and I couldn't wait till lunchtime. You also received enough change to buy some lollies, it was great.

Those were the days when things seemed to be so easy. I would walk home after school, but wouldn't always go straight back home. Sometimes I would go to a mate's house. It used to be interesting as you entered the house, there would be all sorts of food and cooking aromas, it was so different from our home. I could smell garlic, basil and salami.

Some of the kids use to keep pigeons and chickens as pets, which I thought was a bit different as I only had a pet dog, and mum had a cat. I would go home and tell mum all about how different those people were and asked if she would make me some spaghetti. She would say, "Sure, Mick, here you go." She would open up a can and make me some toast to go with it. I had to laugh. I thought, *'That's not what my mate gave me at lunch today.'*

Mum was a good cook. She cooked all the Australian meals :roast meat and vegetables, sausages and vegetables and on Fridays we would get a treat, fish and chips and desserts would sometimes be apple pie or scones. Mum learnt how to cook from Nan. Nan was Scottish, and Pop was English so we would eat foods familiar to those countries. As I grew older, I loved trying different foods from all over the world.

Chapter 4

HORSES

My fondest childhood memories were when I was between the ages of eight to eleven years old. As I remember, these were the most enjoyable times I had. On the weekends I would hang out at the horse riding school, which was not far from my school.

You could hire a horse for an hour for one dollar and twenty cents, using no saddle, jump on and off. It would take about an hour to ride the horse around the track that we had to follow. The track would take you down to the back beach where the wheat silos were, past the football oval and across to the front beach and back to the riding school.

An old guy ran the local horse riding school. Everyone thought he was a dirty old perve. He would invite young girls that were about fourteen to sixteen years old into his house. An hour later, they would come out and get a horse ride for free. They were able to use it for as long as they wanted. I used to wonder what they were doing in there. Later on, I found out he would do sexual things with them. For them to stay quiet, he'd let them use the horses for free.

He gave me the creeps. But I hung around there until my favourite horse came in. I always put my hand up to get that white horse; the mare was fifteen hands high. The horse

Horses

loved running through the water, so we used to go to the beach. I loved and treated the horse as if it were my own.

It felt so good when I was riding. I'd go home and say to mum, "Can I have a horse? Please?" Mum would say we can't; we don't have that kind of money." So I started to do odd jobs, such as the paper round, which was delivering newspapers to local houses to get a little extra cash. That way, I could take the horse out for longer than just an hour; sometimes, I would be out riding the whole day, which I thoroughly enjoyed.

If I weren't horse riding, I'd go to a paddock which was alongside the railway line. It had a few old cars laying around, all rusted with smashed windows, and they sat where they broke down. Sitting under these big willow trees, which were everywhere, we would turn these old cars into cubby houses, and I would meet up with mates. Some girls would hang out there too.

Some of my mates rode their trail bikes on the tracks, there were some good jumps, I'd watch them riding, but I wasn't into bikes. I had a few rides, but after a couple of nasty falls, it put me off.

A couple of my mates were smoking cigarettes and asked me if I wanted a puff, I said, "okay." It made me feel cool. So, from that time on I started to smoke cigarettes. I would sneak smokes out of my mum's packet until one day she caught me, she went off her head because I was only about eleven, but I didn't listen, my mates did it, and I wanted to fit in.

Things at home were starting to go back downhill. Mum was drinking again, and she would often have friends over. When Eddie would come home from work, she would be half drunk. That would annoy him, which I understood because I never liked it.

It was not because she was a bad drunk; she would play records and sing and appeared happy. It was the people that would come to our house to drink with her that would piss me off. They would act like dickheads. They drove me mad with their bullshit. Sometimes there would be fights, and that would scare me. I would take off and look for my mates.

Eddie's brother Fred used to come over a lot. When he got drunk, he would talk about jail and crimes. I found it interesting and thought he was cool. It's easy to be impressed by adults when you're a kid. Fred would sometimes be carrying a gun in his jacket, which impressed me.

He was involved with the Painters and Dockers in Melbourne. You wouldn't want to mess with any of these guys. They controlled the dockyards and were involved in organised crime. Throughout my teens, he would let me tag along with him in his car and go into the city where he would meet some shady people.

Later on, I would ask Fred who they were. He would tell me some of them were very well-known in the media for being big-name criminals. From that time on, I was always interested in that lifestyle. They had the money, the nice cars and could have anything they wanted. I'd go home and tell mum. But she wasn't impressed with me hanging out with my uncle. Mum would tell Fred not to take me to those places, but he never listened.

One place he would take me was in North Melbourne where they'd play Two-Up. I couldn't go in being underage, so he'd say, "Sit in the car and wait." To pass the time I would play the tape player and listen to music. As I waited, I watched lots of people entering and leaving the building, until the cops came and raided it. I saw all of these guys come running out. I felt that this was exciting to watch.

When Fred came outside, he jumped into the car and raced off at high speed to get as far away as possible. I asked who was there. He mentioned some names, like; Mick Gatto, Chopper Reid, and some other heavyweight guys. Later on, these men would be household names of the under-belly world.

Chapter 5

FIRST CRIME

One night while we had a feed at a pizza shop, Fred asked me if I'd like to earn some cash. I said, "Yeah, what would I be doing?" He said that all I had to do is climb through a window and open the back door and then sit in the van. It seemed easy enough, so I said, "Okay."

We drove down a dark alley in Footscray, a few suburbs from where I lived. As we went down the lane, I noticed that there were high fences on both sides. There were some houses in this alley, but there were mostly businesses in the path.

Fred pulled up and said, "It's that fence there, I'll be waiting at the back door. See that window, climb up and see if you can open it with this jimmy bar."

I said, "Yeah, I'll give it a go." I climbed up to the ledge and much to my surprise the window opened quickly.

After climbing through the window, I hopped down and went to the back door and opened it. Fred said, "See those bags hanging over there, grab them and take them out to the van." Nodding, I did what he asked. When I went back inside the building, Fred had more bags at the back door ready for me to load into the van.

First Crime

The building was a suit hire shop. So here I am helping Fred to rob this place, it was such a buzz. Yeah, I was scared as shit with my heart racing. I wondered what would happen if we got caught, but after twenty minutes, which seemed much longer, we were loaded and gone.

Leaving the place, my uncle looked at me and said, "You did well." We headed over towards Carlton, when we arrived at this house, Fred told me to wait while he went inside. Ten minutes later, he came out with a big, mean-looking guy wearing a suit.

I was sitting quietly in the front seat of the car as they approached the back of the van. Fred opened a bag and showed him the suits and jackets. The guy pulled out a roll of cash, handed it over to Fred and they unloaded while I sat there. I wasn't allowed to help or enter this house, so I sat and waited.

After twenty minutes, Fred got in the van and gave me a hundred dollars. I couldn't believe it; It was about the same amount that my stepfather Eddie would make in a week.

I said, "Are you sure, Fred?"

He said, "You did well. Don't spend it all at once."

Later on, when I got home, I hid the money in my room and laid on my bed. Thinking about how I was going to spend that money, I was so excited I couldn't sleep. I was up all night with my head still buzzing.

The next day I wanted to meet up with one of my mates and tell him. I thought better of it as it might get back to my uncle and he would get very pissed off. I just wanted to spend the money but not sure how without mum getting suspicious.

So, I told mum a story that while I was walking home from school, I found a wallet on the ground, saw this money in it, took it and threw the wallet away. Mum said, "Finders, keepers, but you can give me twenty dollars of it." I was okay with that and mum was happy, she had some cash. I could spend the money any way I wanted to, without worrying about anything.

Heading off to town, I went to the sports shop and bought some new footy boots as I didn't own any, and I bought some smokes and lollies. In those days, buying cigarettes at your local shop was easy, even though it was against the law.

Most shops sold to kids, you just had to tell them it was for your mum. Years later, the law changed stopping you from doing this. I started smoking at the age of twelve, which was so stupid, but it was cool to everyone, not like now, I am glad the laws have changed.

My mates noticed I was cashed up and it didn't take long for them to hang around me. They wanted something, so I bought smokes for them. I only had a small group of mates that I hung with; they were Ray, Rob, Mark, Joey, Danny and Steve. Ray was the kind of person who would try to take charge of everything, a real leader. He would even tell older kids what to do, and they would do it.

Later in his life, Ray became a boss of a large organised crime gang of the western suburbs which I'll go into later. Mark was my favourite mate; he proved to be so loyal to me, the others I didn't like as much. Rob was the troubled one; he later turned into a drug abuser.

Danny was the best looking of all of us. He was a real chick magnet. Joey was the smallest one of us but was the funniest; he was also accident-prone. We did everything

First Crime

together. There were a lot of others who hung around with us, some older.

I preferred to hang around the older guys. They made me feel safer, and I looked up to them. They would get into fights and had a reputation in our neighbourhood that it was better to stay away from them.

You would hear people tell stories and brag about them; they were stories that involved them regarding their crimes or fights. Everyone knew who they were. Looking back, I think of how stupid I was to be impressed by these kinds of people. All it did was to lead me down this path.

Mum was drinking once again, more and more and wasn't even aware of me or what I was doing. I was getting away with too much, and I was skipping school. I was catching the train into the city and hanging out instead of going to school. My mates and I would meet up.

We thought that if we went to the city, we wouldn't be seen or caught for not being at school; plus the city felt like a cool place. It was so busy and a big place. It felt as if you were just a speck amongst the crowd.

We would go into Myers and steal things like jeans, jackets and records. If you didn't keep it, you would sell it to a mate. Some days we would catch the tram down to St. Kilda to hang at the beach or go to the ice-skating rink. It was good fun learning how to skate, but I did find it a little hard, though.

The Queen Victoria markets were the best; I loved going there and trying the food. I tried some of the tastiest doughnuts that I have never eaten there. We would wander around the place until it was time to go home because it would be getting close to the end of the school day at 3 p.m.

Chapter 6

GEORGE'S

Arriving home, I would find mum drunk with her friends, and they were behaving very loud. It would piss me off so I would go to my room. Sometimes I would escape to the paddock where some of my friends would normally be. They too had their reasons to get away from home.

Rob would be there because his father would get drunk and beat him and he would see his mother get beaten up so he would take off. Same with Ray, who said he had the same problem. I didn't know about the others, why they came, they didn't say, but I guess they had similar reasons. We would sit around watching some of the older kids riding their dirt bikes.

Near the entrance of the paddock, there was an old house where an old bloke named George lived. The house was a weatherboard home with hardly any paint left on it. There were rusty old cars around the yard and a couple of old sheds, he would let us kids hang around there. It was a meeting spot for us.

George would always have loaves of unsliced bread, with big tins of jam and tins of Milo on the table. He would let us help ourselves. We would sit there eating toast, drinking Milo and chatting to George about anything.

George's

George had horse paintings on his walls, which he painted himself; he was talented. He had a couple of club lounges. I'd sit on the arms and look out of the lounge-room window watching for anyone else entering the paddock. George would have been in his seventies, he was easy to talk to, but I never understood why he would let these kids meet and hang around his place.

At an early age, I understood that where there are boys, there are girls. There were a few rough girls that would go to George's. One girl I remember was a girl named Sandra. She was disgusting. She was a large sandy-haired girl with big tits and a foul mouth. It would be; 'fuck this, fuck that.'

Sandra was around sixteen, a few years older than me. A couple of times I turned up at George's calling out to see if he was home, there'd be no answer. I walked down the hallway and knocked on his bedroom door. There was still no answer, so I'd go to the kitchen and make myself some toast and Milo as I usually would.

After five minutes or so, George came out of the bedroom, grumpier than usual.

He said, "Morning, Mick, what are you doing today?"

He continued talking to me, but I felt as though he wasn't happy to see me. About twenty minutes later, Sandra came out of the bedroom and said, "How the fuck are you, Mick?"

Even though I was young, I felt it was a little strange, her leaving his room. George would buy horse food and blankets for her, whatever she wanted. I often wondered why, but later on, I did work it out.

Sandra used to enjoy stirring us younger guys. There could be four or five of us sitting around the lounge. She would say, "Which one of you guys is going to fuck me?"

We would tell her to fuck off.

One day she was sitting there wearing her school uniform, she pulled her dress up and started using a pushbike pump, sexually on herself, saying 'come on boys.' Shocked at what she was saying, my jaw dropped, thinking, *'You dirty bitch.'* George had two dogs, one was a Kelpie called Rusty, and the other was a Labrador called Bruno.

Sandra would grab their dicks and pull them, saying, "Look, he likes it."

Leaving there feeling disgusted, I thought she was weird.

Sometimes she would come over to my place to say hello to mum. She would walk in and say, "Hi Alice, what are you doing?" Mum didn't mind her, but I would take off whenever she was around.

She would say to mum, "What's wrong with Mick? He can sit on my lap if he likes and kisses me." I would say, 'Fuck off.' And mum would tell her to leave me alone.

My sister had a pony bought for her by Barry, a friend of my mum's. Barry was a big guy. He was always coming around, pissed half the time because he had been at the pubs all day.

After the pubs, he would come over to our house and get on the drink with mum. Barry was a cowboy who played Johnny Cash records, loved John Wayne movies and would wear riding boots.

My sister would get all of the loose change that he had in his pockets, and when she wanted a pony, he bought her one. I thought *'What about me?'* I wanted a horse, but no one bought one for me.' All through my sister's life, I found that she could worm anything out of a man.

Sandra would go across the road, where she kept her pony. He was a grey colour. His name was Dusty. She would say to me, "Check this out, Mick." She would be underneath the pony, licking his dick. I told her to leave him alone, but she would say he was enjoying it. I would tell mum about this. Mum would yell out to Sandra to leave him alone; that's the kind of girl she was.

Sandra had a brother, Peter. He would also stop into George's place. He was a good-looking guy, about seventeen or eighteen and always had girls hanging off him. Peter looked a bit like David Cassidy. The actor and singer of the television show 'The Partridge Family.'

The girls would love Peter, until one day he showed up, dressed up as a girl and carrying a handbag. He'd say, "George, my name is now Tracy!" I sat there thinking, *'What the fuck?'* So, from then on, we called him Tracy.

Being young and naïve, I was a bit confused about Tracy, but I just watched and thought, *'Why would you do that?'* There was another day when he turned up with his boyfriend, Kim. He was a brother of one of my mates. He had boobs and was wearing lipstick. They were both sitting there talking to George about how much they loved each other and going on and on. I just left thinking, *'This is too weird for me.'*

It wasn't long before I stopped going to George's, so did a lot of my mates. Other people started going there that we also thought were a bit too weird. More rough girls were going there, and George was now acting kind of funny with us. Later in life, when I found out what a pedophile was, I reckon George was one; I am glad I stopped going there!

One Friday, we were sitting around bored, one of the guys said, "Why don't we go to the place next to the church?" It was a hall where kids could get together to have fun and organised by a teacher and a priest. They had a pool table and tables and chairs set up with biscuits and drinks. It operated between the hours of 5 p.m. and 9 p.m.

They played music there, and it was somewhere you could hang out, a place to keep kids off the streets. Your parents knew where to find you and wouldn't have to worry. It sounded like a good idea, but I'm not sure it helped much. It became more of a place for us to meet up and work out what we could get up to later.

The following Friday, I decided to go and see how it was. I went to meet up and would hang around for an hour or so. There were a few of what you would call good kids, but more troubled kids.

Things would sometimes get out of control with fights occurring and things would get smashed or broken. The cops would come, and we would take off, this went on for a couple of years. I'm pretty sure it closed down because there were too many fights and bad things happened there.

A few of us would get together, mostly the same bunch and we would wander the streets all night and wouldn't go home until the next day. I would tell mum I was sleeping over at a mate's and she would say, see you later.

One Friday night after a meeting at the hall, we decided to steal a car. We walked around until we saw one to break in to, somehow, we got it started, and off we went cruising around half the night. I was only thirteen and was a little worried about the consequences, but didn't show it to the others, the oldest who was fifteen didn't even seem to give a damn.

We drove to a pizza shop. The time was about midnight. We had a feed and were sitting in the car like it was our home. When we started to head back to where the car

George's

was parked originally, we suddenly heard a siren and saw flashing lights as they were approaching us.

Mark was driving, he was only fourteen, and he was a great driver. While the cops were chasing us, I was in the back seat, shitting myself. We ended up on a block of land with high grass all around us. Mark drove like our life depended on it. We were hitting bumps, and rocks were flying around everywhere. I thought we were going to crash.

I was looking out the back window watching the cop car behind us. It was a fair way back as they must have also been having trouble with the rough track, as dirt bikes only ever used it. This chase lasted for about five minutes but seemed like thirty minutes.

Mark stopped the car and told us to bolt. So, we all hopped out and ran into the thick scrub and laid there as we watched the cops pull up and walk around the EK Holden car. As their headlights were on it, we could see some of the damage around it. The owner of the vehicle would have been upset when they got it back.

We laid there to get our breath back for a few minutes, then slowly got up and walked away, staying quiet so the cops would not hear us. We started walking back into town. It would have had to be a five-kilometre walk all the way, but we kept our eyes peeled checking each car that came past in case it was the cops.

We all went our own way and started to head home. As I was walking home, I grabbed some milk and bread to take with me. I knew where and when the milkman delivered the milk to all the houses around my neighbourhood.

Some Friday nights I would wait outside the dairy for the milkman to load his cart, it was horse-drawn. The horse would tow the cart. I would jump on to help the driver deliver the milk on his round. He would start around midnight until about 6 a.m. He would give me a few bottles to take home.

I was helping the milkman filled in the time at night. I knew where to find the houses where the milk would be at their front door. I grabbed a couple of bottles and moved on to the bakery where they made the bread.

The bakery vans would deliver to all the shops. I would wait out the front across the road from the bakery. As soon as they were loaded I'd run across and open the door of the van, grab a couple of loaves of bread and bolt.

Mum would be just waking up as I got home. She would say "Thanks, Mick, for the milk and bread, I'll make you breakfast." After breakfast, I would go to bed and sleep half the day. Mum knew where I got the milk and bread but didn't say anything. She turned a blind eye to a lot of things that I got up to, but my stepfather Eddie would kick my ass if he knew.

Eddie was a good man. He always worked hard and did things the honest way, because he saw his brother Fred go to jail so many times and had to visit him. Eddie always said to me "If you ever get locked up, I will help you once, but after that, you are on your own." I always kept that in mind.

Around that time, Fred was in jail for a robbery he did, so I didn't see him for a couple of years. That meant no more easy money for a while. Well, that's what I thought. It wasn't too long before Rob, Ray and I did a couple of break-ins to get some cash. Mark would never get involved in that kind of thing as he was more sensible.

Chapter 7

BOYS HOME

About a year went by, and I was still doing little crimes with my mates, breaking into shops or factories, stealing just enough to buy smokes or pay to see a footy game and cover my drinks and a feed.

This one day, we broke into a house, climbing through the back window when suddenly we heard dogs, the owner was home and sent his dogs after us. They were two big German Shepherds, they chased us, and one grabbed me and brought me to the ground the other got Rob and Ray got away.

The man who owned the house told us to freeze, and then the dogs won't bite us. I was shitting myself. The man then rang the cops, and they soon came and put us into the back of the police wagon. They took us to the police station, separated us into different rooms and started to question us.

The cop who was interviewing me began to scare me by saying I was going to jail. The cop hit me with a thick phone book around my head and bent my fingers, asking about some local robberies. He wanted to know if we knew anything about them. I said, "no," even though I did know about some of them, I knew I would be better off if I kept my mouth shut. I was told by my Uncle Fred to say nothing. Sitting there, feeling scared, I said nothing. It wasn't long after that; mum showed up asking what I had done.

Mum started to sweet talk them by saying that I had never been in trouble before and that I was a good boy and was probably following my mates. The copper said that they would have to charge me first then after that, I could go home. Rob wasn't going anywhere as he already had a police record.

Rob already had charges against him; so he went off to a boy's home. I went home and said to myself - never again. But it didn't take long before I did a break-in again and got caught. This time I was going to a boy's home.

When I went to court for the first charge, the judge brought up new charges involving me along with a report from the school saying that I was always fighting and wouldn't behave. The judge then said that maybe going to a boy's home for a while might open my eyes. He gave me three months in the boys' home. I remember mum was standing there crying and that upset me seeing her like that.

Leaving the courthouse, I was transported by a van to the boys' home. Feeling worried about what I was going to happen; I arrived at the boy's home. Getting out of the van all I could see was a twelve-foot red brick wall all around me with barbed wire around the top.

Standing in line with a few other boys and this guy came out in a suit, he stood in front of us and welcomed us to this place. He went through some rules and told us to stay in line and march towards this building, where they told us to undress and have a shower.

We had to pick up some clothes, put them on, carry our blanket and pillow and follow them to another building where we were to sleep.

"Now make your bed," yelled this screw. I had never made a bed before, mum had always done it, and so I made it as best I could, so did the other boys. There were rows of beds in the room, already made, about thirty of them.

I could hear boys yelling, playing footy outside. Suddenly a screw came over and asked me, "Is this how you make your bed?"

I said, "yeah."

"Don't yeah me, say Yes, Sir. Now I will show you how to make your bed, and you will make it the same way every time. Every morning I will be checking your bed. If it's not the same way as I showed you, You will have no breakfast!"

'Oh my god,' I thought, so I watched him and so did the others. Thinking, *'I guess I won't be getting breakfast. I will never remember this way he wants me to make my bed.'*

After we made our beds, he told us what time everything was and where we had to be. We headed to the dining room. There were all these other boys looking at us and saying things to us. It was hard to hear because they were all talking at once. Suddenly I heard a familiar voice, "Mick, hey Mick." It was Rob. I thought to myself, *'Thank God I know someone else in here.'*

Rob came over and said, "You finally got caught. What are you in here for?" I told him, and he then asked me to come and sit with him, I was okay with that. He already had guys sitting with him and seemed to be the leader of them because they all looked to him when he spoke.

Rob introduced me to about six of them. I couldn't remember their names as my head was spinning with everything that was going on. I ended up having my lunch and asked Rob what we do next. He then said, "Just hang with me, and you will be fine."

For the rest of the day, we sat around until dinner time. Shortly after dinner, it was bedtime, which was 6 p.m., and the lights were turned off at 7 p.m. I lay there having trouble sleeping. I could hear the other boys whispering to each other. I was wondering about how I was going to cope and what was happening at home.

The next morning around 5:30 am a screw came in yelling at everyone to wake up and be ready for roll call in twenty minutes. So, we had to get our beds made for starters. I thought to myself, *'Great how's this going to go.'* Getting up and making my bed, I thought I did a good job. The screw came in and checked my bed. He said, "What's this? Well, you can stay here and try again." He called out the roll. Everyone else headed off for their breakfast while I tried to make my bed again.

After remaking the bed, I waited for the screw to come back. As the screw walked in and said, "I hope your bed is made to my standards now." He had a look and then said, "Well, no way, go out to the oval and don't bother going to the hall to have breakfast." My thoughts were, *'That I would starve at this rate.'*

So I headed to the oval where the screws gave us exercises to do. The exercises consisted of star jumps, push-ups etc. I was feeling weak from not eating. My thoughts were on the lines of, *'I have to learn to make my bed properly.'*

After our exercises, we all had jobs to do, I had the job of mopping the floors everywhere, which takes about two hours, then you had an hour to mingle and do what you wanted. I noticed this boy around my age was getting picked on by this big kid; he looked about fourteen and had a couple of mates with him.

This boy was so scared. He looked like a nerd with glasses, who read all the time. He was about three beds up from me, so I went over to him and said, "Hey mate, you want those bullies to stop harassing you?"

He said, "Yes, but how?"

I said, "I'll make a deal with you. Each morning for the rest of my time here, about three months, you make my bed, and I'll sort out your problem." He agreed.

We went to lunch. We had fish fingers and mashed potatoes. I was starving. I ate as though I was starving. After we ate lunch, we had to go to a classroom where we had maths and English. I thought by being here, we wouldn't have to do schoolwork, but no, I wasn't that lucky. We did about two hours of work, after that we could play games like cards and chess. I wanted to have a game of chess. I had seen a kid who was good at it and asked if he could show me how to play.

While playing chess, I noticed one of the bullies heading to the toilet. I thought to myself, *'Here is my chance.'* I followed him, he sat down on the toilet and started pushing out a crap. I noticed no-one around, so I grabbed the steel bucket I had used that morning and went through the door where he sat.

I hit him about three or four times across his head. He couldn't get off the toilet as he was in the middle of his crap. As I hit him, I told him that if he ever picked on that kid with the glasses again, I would hunt him down and he would cop it not just from me but everyone I could get to hit him.

I quickly walked back to my seat and acted as if nothing had happened and said: "Okay, what were you showing me?" Well the bully never went near that kid again, and I had my bed made for me each morning, and the nerdy kid sat with us.

Rob came over a day or so later and asked me what I had done to that bully? He said that the bully's mates said that I was crazy, and to stay away from me. I told him what had happened, he laughed and said, that's the way, buy favours. I thought, *'Yeah, I will, every time I needed something done, I would find a way to get it done.'*

A week went by before mum came to visit me. Mum asked, "How's things, are you being good?" "Yes," I said. She told me that I might get out early if I stayed out of trouble. Mum was right because after eight weeks I was let out early, but Rob was still going to be there for a while longer.

It felt good to hop in the car and head home away from there. When I got home, mum had a great feed for me and even dessert. Mum asked if I thought I had learned anything from being there. She was hoping that I was going to stay out of trouble. I said to myself that I wouldn't break into any places again.

The next day I went out to find Ray, Mark, Steve, Joey and Danny to tell them about it all.

Here they were down the beach riding their push bikes.

They came up to me and said, "Hey, you out! How was it?"

I explained to them how horrible it was, then said I was going for a swim, it was so good to hop in the water and catch some waves, I felt I was washing everything away and putting it behind me.

Around this time mum and Eddie were wanting to sell the house and move to Footscray, which was about five suburbs away, thinking if I stayed away from my mates, I would stay out of trouble. They sold up, and we moved. I hated the idea.

Chapter 8

MOVE TO FOOTSCRAY

The new house was on the main road called Ballarat Road, it was a very busy road, and I didn't like it. Mum told me that I had to go to a new school as well. I thought, *'Great. I won't go!'* Mum took me there to enrol me. But from day one I never turned up, although Mum thought I was going. I used to get up and wonder, *'What am I going to do each day to fill in the time?'*

Footscray was so different, at Williamstown, there were beaches, paddocks and wheat silos to hang around. I knew everyone as well, and Williamstown was such a better place. Footscray was more of an industrial area, with a lot of mixed races and a much tougher area and a bit scary.

I caught the train to Williamstown most days and tried to catch up with mates. I would often see them heading to school and tried to talk them into hanging with me instead. Usually, someone did, and we would head into the city.

Eventually, I stopped going down there and started to meet new friends in the Footscray area. After about four months, the new school rang my mum and asked if I was still transferring to their school. Mum told them that I should have already been there, but they had never seen me. Well, I was well and truly busted!

About 3.30pm, I arrived home as usual, and mum asked if I had enjoyed school that day. I told her that it was okay. Mum said to me that she had received a call and found out that I had never been there. Asking where I had been, I came clean and told her the truth.

"Wait until Eddie gets home, he won't be happy with you!" Mum said. *'Great,'* I thought.

When Eddie arrived home, Mum told him what I had been doing. He just said, "Oh well, if you want to be an uneducated bum and not go to school, you will just end up in jail, and nothing will become of you." *'Blah, blah, blah,'* I thought and just took off. The next day mum told me to get in the car because she was taking me to school. *'Oh my god,'* I thought, and off we went.

We pulled up at the school, and she walked me to the front door and said, "Now you head in." So I did. I went to the head master's office and knocked on the door.

He said, "Yes, what can I do for you?"

I told him my name and that I had been attending Williamstown Tech.

He was looking around his desk to find the paperwork and asked how long ago I was transferred. I replied about four months ago. He remembered.

"You are the kid that I was talking to your mum about yesterday?"

I said, "Yes."

"Well, where have you been?"

I just told him that I had been hanging in the city. He said, "Well, I will take you to your class, where you can start, but before we go, I want to give you some rules that

Move to Footscray

we go by." I wasn't listening. All I could think was, *'I hate this already.'*

After going through the rules, we went to a classroom, where he introduced me to the teacher. All I did was look around at the students thinking, *'This is going to be tough.'* This school had a reputation of a lot of fights, bad kids that played up and the teachers were always being hit and abused. I sat at my seat, and within one hour, we had to move to our next class, we did this every hour. I got lost a lot as I had a kid showing me around at first, but he pissed off after a while. I was left to find my way around.

It didn't take long before I looked lost and out of place. "Who are you? Where did you come from?" They said. Soon I was challenged by this kid for a fight. I was alone and worried about how I would handle this situation.

As soon as the bell went to finish the last class, I walked out the back gate, which led to an oval. As I went through the gate, sure enough, there was this guy with his mates. He started to push me around. I told him that I didn't want any trouble, but the guy king-hit me. I threw a few punches, but he was getting the better of me, and in that split second, I thought, *'If I lose, I will cop it every day.'*

Noticing a kid standing nearby with a cricket bat, I snatched it off him, and I started laying into the kid that was beating me. I swung it around saying, "Come on you cunt!"

I took a few swings, he started bleeding, and a few of his mates came towards me. I swung it at them and said, "Come on, I'll take you all out."

They all started to run. I turned around to see a teacher watching. He called out and told me to go with him to the headmaster's office. He wasn't happy, the first day there and I was already in a fight, but it wasn't my fault. The headmaster rang mum to come down to the school.

I sat outside his office until mum arrived, she went in and spoke to him. After ten minutes, she came out. We drove home. She was harping on about it. I was sitting there not listening, thinking, *'How I was going to get through the next day?'*

The next day as I walked through the gate, I was panicking. I got to my first class, and a couple of other kids started to talk to me. At lunchtime, I walked out of the gate with them, and we headed to the fish and chip shop. While I was at the shop, I noticed the kid that I had fought yesterday there. He looked at me but didn't say anything.

After getting my food, we sat outside the shop, eating and talking. They told me about the fight and said they were talking about it around the school. They must have thought I was nuts the way I used the cricket bat, I was thinking, *'Really?'*

Later that day, I was walking home thinking about the fight. It seemed to me that every time I had fought in the past, I had often lost control and become so violent that it went too far. It showed everyone that I act so crazy, but nobody hassled me again.

Growing up, it proved to work for me, but people would say 'One day you will kill someone and you will end up in jail.' I used to think about that a bit at times, and I concluded I probably would be.

Chapter 9

WOLFMAN

After attending a month or so at this new school, I hated every day. One afternoon I was walking home, which would usually take about thirty minutes. I noticed a guy washing a motorbike out the front of this house on the lawn. It caught my eye, and I thought, *'What a nice bike.'* The guy looked about twenty or so. He had red hair, really rough looking.

I said as I walked past, "Nice bike mate."

He turned and said, "Yeah thanks."

The next few days, I would walk past and would see this bike parked outside his house. He was always doing something to it. The house was one of those housing commission homes, run-down, and probably built in the sixties.' I could hear his mum calling out. It sounded like he had brothers and sisters.

He looked at me one day and said, "Where do you go to school?" I told him, and he then asked how long I had been there. "A few months and hating it," I said. He asked me why. I replied because I came from Williamstown. I don't know anyone here, and no-one wants to get to know me.

He told me anytime I wanted to pop in, I could. I thought that was cool as he was five years older than me for one reason. I went home and told mum I met this guy who owns a bike and has a patch on his back, he must ride for a gang. Mum just gave me this look as if to say 'great another crim for me to hang out with.' She was too busy drinking listening to her music or having her friends over.

The next day I thought, *Fuck going to school, I'm going to call over to that bikie guy's place.* I walked up to his driveway to the front door and knocked. The door swung open. His mum was standing there with a smoke hanging out of her mouth.

She shouted out to me, asking me who I was. I asked her if the guy who owns the bike was home. She looked at me and yelled, "Yeah, he's around the back asleep, go through the side gate." I said, "thanks," and went through the gate and out to the back.

There was a bungalow at the back, and his bike was outside. Walking up to the door, I knocked and said, "hello," but there was no answer. I knocked again.

I heard a voice yell out, "Is that you mum? Piss off!" I felt a bit scared now.

I called out "Hi, it's me, the guy you spoke to yesterday."

He told me to hang on a minute, the door opened with the red-headed guy standing there in his jocks. He recognised me and told me to come in.

Walking in there, I noticed the room was a mess. There were clothes, old pizza boxes, ashtrays full of butts and empty beer cans everywhere. "Don't worry about the mess; grab a seat." The guy said as I was looking around to find somewhere to sit while he went and got some clothes.

Next minute he came out and asked me to pass him the bong.

Wolfman

I said, "Okay, what's a bong?" I had never seen one before. He told me it was on the table; I looked, and there was this bottle with a hose on top of it. I said, "Is this it?"

He said, "Yes, pack it for me." I saw a bowl full of chopped weed, and I packed it before handing it over to him. He took a big toke and said, "That feels better."

He introduced himself, "I'm Steve, otherwise known as Wolfman, and you are?"

I said, "I'm Mick."

"Cool, You want a cone?" He said.

I said, "I only smoke cigarettes, I have never had pot before."

He replied, "That's cool mate, well, it's there if you want one."

I looked and thought, *'Nah, I probably would look silly to him if I coughed and carried on.'*

He said, "What can I do for you, anyway?"

I said, "Nothing, I just didn't want to go to school today and thought I would come to see you and hang out."

He said, "Well that's okay, I'm just sitting here today getting stoned. I'm waiting on a couple of mates to show."

I was cool with that, so I just hung there with this guy called Wolfman and asked him what his mates' names were. He said names like Crazy horse, Caveman and Mongo. These guys must be really scary to have names like this, but it was their bikie names.

We sat and chatted for a while; talking about what I got up to and about how crazy things are at home. He told me a few stories about himself, and it made me more comfortable being there. It was getting close to the end of school hours.

I told him I had better go but would catch up with him again. He was cool with that and told me I could drop in anytime. Walking home feeling good about myself; it felt great to be a kid hanging with an older guy that rode a motorcycle in a gang.

The next few weeks, I hung with Steve instead of going to school. I started smoking pot. Steve suggested that if I wanted to make some cash, I should see if any of my mates would like some pot and that he would supply it.

The next day I went down to Williamstown and saw a couple of my mates and asked if they wanted to do some dealing for me, they were keen. Once a week I would take some deals to them and be back every few days to collect the cash, it sounded easy.

The next couple of days I went back with an ounce, all in single deals and handed about five to each mate, they would make about five dollars on each deal, I would make around the same.

After about two weeks, I gave up, as I found it too much of a hassle. One mate spent the cash. One didn't sell any of the five bags I gave him. A waste of time it seemed, travelling time alone was about an hour on public transport each way, a bit of a pain, but I did like the idea of dealing and getting money.

The trouble with mates selling for you, if they stuffed you around, you would have to get heavy-handed with them, and I didn't want to do that. I thought it was better to use them for muscle instead. I did get into dealing when I was about nineteen years old, but at this time, I just wanted to do other things. I told Steve that I was sorry, but I didn't want to sell at the moment, he was cool about it.

Wolfman

Steve's bikie mates would give me the shits, so I stopped going around there. They could be nice, but other times they would get too rough with me, treating me like a bitch, which I didn't like. It was like an initiation for the new guys, and I wasn't going to be one of their bitches, plus I wasn't interested in joining them, and I wasn't that much into bikes.

I thought, *'Now what will I do with my time? I don't want to go to school, and I'm not going around Steve's, I felt that I would tell mum that I wanted to leave school.'* Mum was okay with it as long as I got a job.

Well, I headed down to the meatworks where you had to turn up each morning at the gate and wait to be called to work for the day. After four days turning up, I got on. It was a real eye-opener to see animals being killed and broken down. I got used to it quickly, but I didn't like it.

I only lasted about a month and thought the job just wasn't for me, so I didn't bother going anymore. Mum was on my back to get out of bed and get a job or go back to school. I didn't want that.

On Friday nights mum would have a few drinks with a couple of guys who were tow truck drivers. Mum knew them from years ago, and they would come over and hang at the house. Usually, a couple of friends of hers would be there as well. The tow truck boys loved sitting there listening to mum and her friends getting drunk.

We lived on a busy corner on Ballarat Road where there were always four or five accidents a week and Friday nights were always the busiest. The tow truck boys offered me thirty dollars for each car they towed if I rung them when an accident happened, it was easy money to make on a Friday night.

I would be by the phone waiting for an accident to happen, I would make sixty to a hundred dollars a week. They asked me to go out with them to crashes, it was exciting but also horrible seeing the fatalities.

One story always stayed with me; a lady had overdosed, and her hubby was rushing her to the hospital when he ran a red light and hit a truck. Their car went under its tray, and it took his head off, when we got there, his head was on his lap, the lady survived. I was angry with her, he was trying to help her, and it cost him his life. My job was cleaning up the glass on the road and helping with hooking up the cars etc.

For about two years, I worked with the tow truck drivers. One night we got called out to a smash on the highway, a car had run off the road and hit a tree, the driver had been drinking.

When we arrived, I jumped out and ran to the car to see if the people were alright. As I opened the passenger's door, I saw my cousin, dead, and started crying. My boss asked me what was wrong, and he got the other tow truck driver to take me home. I told my stepfather that his nephew had died, I never went back to doing that job again, but there were so many stories, just on my experiences with those guys, you could write a book.

Chapter 10

STEALING CARS

Around the age of fifteen, I began stealing cars. Every Friday night I would steal three or four cars and take them straight to the smash repair guy's house, about ten kilometres out of town. They would strip the cars for the parts.

I would get two hundred dollars a car and made around six hundred dollars for one night's work. With that, I would buy an ounce of weed and sell deals to my mates, doubling my money. I was bringing in good money for a fifteen-year-old, so why would I bother looking for a real job.

Around the same time, I met this guy called Rob. He asked me if I wanted to make some good cash. I said, "Yeah, doing what?" He said, "Don't muck around with deals and stealing cars. Come with me to Queensland and help pick up pounds of weed and bring it back here, you will make $2,000 a trip." I said, "Yeah, why not!" *I thought it would be exciting getting away from Melbourne for a week.*

Rob was twenty-four years old, and I was just sixteen, I enjoyed hanging with older guys. It made me feel safer because guys my age seem to turn on each other, and I couldn't trust them.

We drove up to Queensland, and at this stage, my mum had left my stepfather and was living up there with a guy named Peter. He was a big man, from Holland originally, but carried on like an Aussie. When mum was first with him, I didn't like him, but as time went on, he didn't seem that bad.

Rob and I arrived to collect the weed at Yeppoon, a coastal town in Queensland. This guy walks up to Rob, shook hands as if they had known each other for years. The guy had a big fishing boat. They were drinking, getting stoned and catching up with old times. I got up and went for a walk to have a look around. When I got back from my walk, we crashed out and ended staying overnight.

The next morning they put two big army bags in the boot of the car, and we headed off back home. I asked Rob if we could stop into my mum's for a couple of hours since I hadn't seen her in a while. Mum's place was at Redcliffe, a bayside suburb with beaches. It was a nice place just north of Brisbane. Mum was happy to see me and asked me to come back up and stay for a while. I told her that I would soon.

We stayed for about two hours and headed off again. We drove back to Melbourne, only stopping for fuel. When we arrived back home, we dropped off the bags, and Rob gave me two thousand dollars. I said, "thanks," and he asked if I was up for another trip again in about a week, I said, "sure."

I thought, *'That was so easy,'* and went out and spent the money on a car to do up; it was an old Charger. I didn't have a license, but that didn't bother me. I still drove it and got my Uncle Fred to help me painting it and doing up the motor. He was out of jail for a while so he could do it for me. Fred was always going in, and out of jail, I lost count of how many times it was.

For a sixteen-year-old, I thought I was doing pretty well. I always had money coming in, and I had a car. A few of my mates, the same age as me, were getting into heroin. It bothered me seeing them sitting there on the nod, not knowing what was happening. It also made me a bit more careful around them, but I would only hang with them at times when I was bored.

I started hanging with a girl called Tracey, she was cute, cheeky and she had a nice smile. I was at her place one day when she told me that her brother was a skinhead with the West Side Sharps; he is now one of the leaders.

Sharps were members of suburban youth gangs in Australia, particularly in Melbourne from the 1960s and 1970s. Sharpies were known for being violent, with a strict moral code. The name comes from their emphasis on looking and dressing 'sharp.' Usually, they'd wear tight jeans, shirts and work boots or Doc Martens boots. They had piercings and shaved or punk haircuts and listened to punk music or reggae.

I thought that she was probably bullshitting me, but she reached over and grabbed some photos of her with her brother and all these skinheads. It was cool because I had heard of them around town but never met them. I asked her, "Would you introduce me to him?"

She answered, "Sure, as long as I tell him you're my boyfriend."

I said, "Sure, but I'm not."

Tracey said, "If I tell him that, he will give you the time; otherwise they will more likely bash you."

"Okay," I said.

Tracey took me to where they hung out. It was at Footscray Park alongside the river near Flemington racetrack. They had a shed there that they used for a hang-out. Tracey walked up to her brother and said, "Keith, this is Mick, my fella." He looked at me and said, "G' day Mick, where you from?" I told him, and he said, "Cool, we know a few boys from there. Would you like to come for a ride into the city with us tonight?" I said, "Yeah, sure. What's in there?"

Keith told me there was a gang there and the more numbers that they had going, the better. I thought, '*This is some test for me so I told him I'd go.*' They were all wearing similar clothes, overalls, heads shaved and earrings etc. They seemed to go on about the white race and how they hated the Vietnamese moving into our area.

Later that night we headed to the station, there would have been about twenty of these skinheads. We got on the train, and within ten minutes Keith started on this guy sitting there not doing anything. Keith punched him, and the others joined in. I was watching, I didn't like what I was seeing but was glad that it wasn't me, so I kept tagging along.

We ended up in the city, and they were hunting down this gang called The Black Dragons. They were along the Yarra River which ran alongside the city. When they saw them, they started running at them. I joined in and threw some punches. I enjoyed it for some reason.

Later coming back on the train Keith introduced me to one of the other leaders. His name was M, just M, he was covered in tattoos and was a real scary kind of man. I knew straight away; you wouldn't fuck with him. We got back to Footscray Station and started walking back to the park when M said he was getting some smokes.

Stealing Cars

I watched as he went into the shop asked for cigarettes and a few other things and just walked out. He didn't even pay for them. Someone pointed out he used stand over tactics on all the shops in this area, and he got what he wanted, or the shop got busted up. He protected them from other gangs trying to stand over them; I was impressed with that.

We ended up back at this old pub which these boys took over. They would be listening to the Sex Pistols and smashing into each other playing pool. It was so full you could hardly move. I liked playing pool. I was good enough to play competition but I would only play for money and I did quite well at that.

Chapter 11

ROMPER STOMPING

The next few months, I hung around with these skinheads who were selling plenty of drugs to the younger members. The older ones weren't into smoking weed. They were heavy drinkers and were against the drug thing. I tried to be careful; I didn't want them finding out what I was doing.

They knew where I was from, and I guess they wanted me to introduce them to some of my mates in Williamstown. I did, it came in handy for them because they were always looking for more numbers when it came to fights with other gangs.

Keith caught on to what I was doing and was getting pissed off with me because the boys would be getting stoned and didn't want to go anywhere; they just wanted to sit back and relax.

Keith came up to me one day and said, "Mick, you either stop bringing your pot here or don't come here at all." I chose not to hang with them anymore, that was fine. I would see them sometimes around town, I'd say G'day but stayed away as I didn't want to upset them.

I headed down to Williamstown for a while to see what was going on. The boys were a bit distant with me because they hadn't seen me in a while, but I got the local gossip on what had been going on. It seemed like I was a bit of a stranger to them, and didn't feel as welcome, so I stopped going down there for a while.

Getting bored being by myself, I started spending some time at my local football club and watching them play. It was the home of the Western Bulldogs. In competition, they were usually around the bottom of the ladder and were a struggling club. I would go there and met a few new friends. They were straight shooters. All the boys had jobs and did the right thing; I liked hanging with these guys; they were different from my other friends.

This one day, I was at a game, and I noticed this girl. She was a cheerleader for the club. I could not take my eyes off her. I noticed that she was also looking at me. So, I went up to her and said, "Hi, what are you doing after the game?"

She said, "Nothing!"

I said, "You want to do something?"

"Sure," she said.

Afterwards, I met her outside, she had a friend with her, and my mate was with me. I liked her friend, so we went to the local bowling alley and hung out there, we ended up kissing, and she ended up being my first serious girlfriend.

She lived on the other side of town. I would drive over to her place and visit her. She'd tell me that I shouldn't be driving because I was underage. I'd laugh and tell her that it was all good.

I would drive her all over the place while doing drop-offs to mates who wanted their pot. She wondered what I was up to and asked me. I didn't want to lie to her. Once she knew, she would try stopping me from doing the wrong things that I enjoyed. I would get angry and argue with her.

One of the blokes I was hanging around with liked her, he started spending more time talking to her, and I wondered if something was going on. One day I told her I thought he was trying to chat her up. She denied that anything was going on. She said that he was listening to her because I was upsetting her with what I was doing by selling drugs, and whatever else I did.

Each time I would see her, this guy would be not far away, he was pissing me off, and it would cause fights between us. One night I was in a public phone box ringing her to find out why she never showed up at a game, and she said she was sick. I started going on about this guy; being jealous is a terrible thing and at that age, you can't control your feelings. It was frustrating, I ended up slamming down the phone and stomped out of the phone box angrily.

I looked up, and there was the guy who had been spending time with my girl. He was walking out of a pizza shop carrying his pizza.

He said, "Hi Mick." I walked up and without saying anything. I king-hit him. He fell back through the shop window. I took off thinking, *'Fuck what did I do?'* I went to a mate's place around the corner and walked in. He said, "What's up?" I told him what happened.

Going into the bathroom to wash my hands, I heard a knock on the door. It was the cops, and they had the shop owner with them. That prick I hit had laid charges against me, and I had to pay for damages for the window. I thought that's not the end of it. I will catch this prick again, bloody dog.

Sure enough a few weeks later, I was out the front of my house, and I saw him walking past on the other side of the road. For some reason, I felt he was snooping around to see if my girlfriend was over mine. When I saw him, I went into a rage and went inside, grabbed my 22 calibre rifle and going back out the front of the house I yelled, "You better run you rat!" I let off a couple of rounds behind him, hitting the fence behind his head.

He ran alright, but just as I was doing that my stepfather pulled up coming home from work. He jumped out of his car and grabbed me, grabbed the gun and said, "What the fuck are you doing?" He hit me and told me to get inside.

Again, he asked me, "What do you think you are doing?" I told him, and he said, "I don't ever want to see you doing that again, especially over a girl, don't be so damn stupid." I listened and decided to go away for a while in case the cops come looking for me. I rang mum and said that I was coming up to Queensland for a while. I was on a plane the next day.

When I arrived in Queensland, mum was still living in Redcliffe. It was a nice place right near the beach. She was glad to see me and was still with this guy Peter. I stayed for about four months. My sister was living with mum. My sister and I had a huge fight one day, and I thought to myself, *'I'm going back to Melbourne.'*

I left, heading back down south, and went back to my stepfather who had moved into a smaller old house. It was okay, but I was feeling down and depressed about everything. I needed to get out and do something, keep myself busy, what it was, I had no idea.

Seventeen years old with no job and wondering what I was going to do with myself. I went to saw my uncle and asked if he had anything for me to do.

He said, "Yes, I have if you're interested." I asked him what it was.

He said it was a warehouse job with boxes of cigarettes. I was happy to give it a go.

A few days later, we were heading to the warehouse in West Footscray. He had a truck that I had never seen before. I guessed it was a stolen truck. We drove there. He told me to hop out, go under the fence, over to the building and break a panel. Once inside I was to go to the desk where I'd see a set of keys in the top drawer.

Here I am thinking, *'How does he know where the keys are?'* I did as he said and the keys were there. I went back outside. The key was for the padlock on the gate, and he locked the gate behind us. Opening the roller door for him, he drove in and started loading these boxes containing cartons of smokes.

Halfway through loading the truck, we heard a car pull up. It was security checking on the place. We stopped moving and listened to him until he left. We continued to load the truck. That's why my uncle locked the gate to show no disturbance. We left with the truck all loaded, went through the gate, leaving it unlocked.

We arrived at my uncle's place and drove into his backyard and unloaded the truck. He said, "You take the cartons out of the boxes, while I get rid of the truck." He returned two hours later in a taxi. I told him that I had done what he had asked. He gave me a bag and told me to load it up with the cartons.

The bag was one of those army sacks. I could put a fair amount in it. "You take that bag home with you and sell them and come back tomorrow with your car, and you can take the rest of the smoke cartons as your share. Now load up the boot," he said. I said, "Okay."

Romper Stomping

The next day I was back with my car loading the boot with the smokes. My uncle was in the yard burning off the cardboard boxes in his forty-four-gallon drum. I said, "thanks," to my uncle and left. Once I arrived home, I started selling the smokes. I forget how much for, but I had no problem getting rid of them as most of my mates smoked

A few days later, I went back to see my uncle, but he wasn't home. My Nan said that he had been taken away by the cops. She told me it was over a robbery; I was shocked. There was a news report on television about it. It was showing pictures of the scene and the pictures of the boxes. The reporter was telling people to keep an eye out for anyone selling stolen cigarettes.

The police found out about it as my uncle was burning the boxes in the yard, the smoke was drifting over to the neighbour's house and he wasn't happy. When he looked over the fence, he saw my uncle burning the boxes. He saw the name of the smokes on it, and he rang the cops and told them. Of course, he never told them that I was involved. My uncle got two years in jail for it.

While my uncle was in jail, I would visit him. He was in Pentridge, a real old school jail made of bluestone. I'd go in to visit him. I could only talk to him over the phone. It was a scary place to be. After a while, he went to a low-security country jail where you could have barbecues and sit outside to talk.

One day as I was leaving, I saw two of my friends in there. I thought, *'Great, is this my future?'* As I was leaving, my uncle told me that there was a box at reception for me to collect. It contained things he had made, teddy bears etc. He wanted me to hand out to the younger family members. I told him 'Okay'.

As I left, my uncle gave me instructions to drive down the hill and turn left at the dirt road. Follow the road for about a kilometre and look to my right. Then go into the paddock where I'd find some magic mushrooms. He was working with some other inmates chopping wood when he saw them.

He thought he would have a feed. Not knowing what they were, he reported to the screw that he felt sick. He was tripping on them. He had never tripped before, so he was freaking out. He said to me that I might like them. I had never had them before but thought why not give them a go.

Once I left, I went to where he said to go and sure enough there they were. I got a bag full, took them home and went over to a mate's place. We boiled them with Milo and 'wow' I was tripping with my mate. I can tell you it's like acid. I said to myself never again, but over the years, I did it again about three more times.

Chapter 12

MEETING SAM

I headed back up to Queensland to go to see mum. Things hadn't changed much. Mum said she was getting married to Peter, and she wanted me to give her away, I said, "Yes." While she arranged the wedding, I was spending my days at the beach.

On one of these days, I noticed two girls in school uniform hanging around the fish and chip shop. One of them had her eye on me. She had long blonde hair and was slim built. So I decided to go over and say hello.

She said her name was Samantha.

I said, "What are you guys doing?"

They said, "We were supposed to be at school, but we took off."

I asked them, "Would you like to hang out with me?"

"Sure," they replied.

We hung at the beach, eating chips and having fun. They had to head home as the bus arrived in the afternoon. So I walked them to the bus stop.

I said to Sam, "Would you like to see me tomorrow?"

"Sure," she said.

The next day I met her, and she was on her own this day. I asked her if she wanted to come back to my place, and she did. Mum met her, and she hung out with me in my room. We listened to music, and from there, things got a bit heated if you know I mean.

Later that afternoon, it was time for her to catch her bus. She asked if I would go with her and walk her home. I obliged. We were on the bus for about half an hour, before we reached her stop, and then I walked her home, which took about another twenty minutes.

When we arrived at her home, I saw that she lived in a two-story house. It had a pool in the yard. I thought, *'Where I come from if you had a pool in your yard, you must be rich.'* But up in Queensland, pools were more common than down south. She told me I could swim if I felt like it, so I did.

After my swim, I went upstairs. Sam made some lunch for me and said, "I am normally here by myself. My dad is always at work or his girlfriend's. He comes home with food and money and leaves again. My brother is nineteen, and he is always out with his mates, he is never home." It was a bit sad her having no one around.

Every day now, I would do the same thing. Meet her after school, go to her place and have a swim. After a few days, I would stay over and go to her school in the morning to drop her off. When I would go home, mum would ask all these questions about where I had been.

One night that I was staying over early the next morning, her dad came home. The bedroom door opened, and her dad was standing there. He said, "Sam, can you come out here?" I could hear them fighting about who I was and what was I doing in her bed.

Meeting Sam

Once I heard him leave, she said, "I think we should go." I was shitting myself, thinking like any dad, he was going to flog me for being in bed with his fifteen-year-old daughter.

Heading back to my place, she went off to school. I didn't see her for a couple of days. Her dad grabbed her and took her to his girlfriend's house. He told her she was to stay there. He was trying to keep her away from me.

After about a week, she turned up at my house. She told me that her dad was keeping her as a prisoner in his girlfriend's house. She just wanted to be with me. I suggested that we run away and that I would take her to Melbourne, where my stepfather lives.

Sam was happy to leave. We stayed the night in a room at a pub and the next day caught a bus back to Melbourne. When we arrived, I rang my stepfather. He told me that he had moved house and was sharing with a mate. But there was a granny flat in the yard that I could have, so I was cool with that. We both moved into the flat, set things up and made it our own little home.

About a week later, I caught up with a few of my mates and introduced Sam to them straight away. She didn't like them. She said that my mates were scary. I'd ask her what she meant. She said that they took drugs and looked terrible. I agreed, but that's all I knew.

Sam came from a nice area in Queensland. She went to a private school, and she had never seen this kind of life before. She started nagging me about them, and I now started going out a lot without her.

After about a month passed, I was getting sick of her. When I get back home, I am going to break up with her, put her on a bus and send her back to Queensland.

When I arrived home, I went to tell her, but she told me that she had some news. She was pregnant, well I thought that was going to change everything. I told her that it was great and I now thought, '*I've got to do the right thing.*' The thought of being a father was exciting.

As time went on, I was still going out with mates doing things like selling drugs, stealing cars and selling them. Sam would tell me to get a real job and stop doing what I was doing.

The money I would get from a proper job was nowhere near the amount I earned selling drugs or stealing cars. I continued doing it. However, she wasn't happy and said she wanted to go back to Queensland to have the baby and that her parents would like that. I agreed, and we headed back up north.

We arrived back in Queensland at Mum's place when she was about four months pregnant. Mum was excited I was going to be a father and also about the fact that she was going to be a grandmother. We shopped for baby stuff during the pregnancy; it was exciting.

We visited Sam's mum. Her name was Wendy. She lived on her own on a property. Looking at her, I thought, '*Wow!*' She was stunning. She was a model who worked at Myers in the makeup section. Her boyfriend who was in jail doing five years for scamming people.

Wendy being a normal mother, asked me questions about myself, and how we met. Sam and I stayed overnight and went home the next day to Mum's house. I noticed Sam and her mum weren't close as they seemed to fight and argue, but we did visit a few more times.

Meeting Sam

Sam was about seven months into her pregnancy. I wasn't working and knew I needed to get cash, but I didn't want to work. I didn't know anyone up here and wanted to get some money quickly. So, I went out one night and stole this car from a car yard.

After I parked it in a quiet place, I had no idea what to do with it. I noticed it had a flash set of mags and thought if I can get them off, I will sell them. Jacking up the car to take off the mags, I realised I had no way of getting them home. So I rang Peter, mum's husband and asked if he could pick me up. I would give him some cash when I sold them. As I was taking the mags off, the cops showed up and busted me.

I ended up in jail that night and mum bailed me out the next morning. Sam wasn't happy with me at all. I explained to her that I was trying to get some cash for the baby. She told me to get a job as everyone else does. I thought *'Fuck that!'* As I wasn't trained in any particular field of work.

At court, they gave me community service, doing mowing at parks etc. Sam went into labour at nine months. I was doing community service, and mum came down and told me that Sam was in the hospital. They were okay to let me go to see her.

When we got to the hospital, I could hear Sam screaming. She had a little girl. We named her April. I was so happy. We took her home the next day, and mum was so excited. We had the cot and all these baby things.

It was hard waking up to feed her, and all the other normal parenting things you do with a new baby. It was a lot to learn, being a first-time father, but mum was such a great help.

Chapter 13

THE CREW

After about six months we went back to Melbourne and found a flat in a place called Altona. It was a nice quiet, country town about twenty kilometres from the city. It had beaches along the coastline of the bay that surrounded it.

Everything seemed quite reasonable for a while. Watching my daughter growing up, I felt good. It wasn't long before I started to get back with my old crew, hanging around them and dealing in weed.

My uncle was out of jail. He started up an escort business and asked me to do some work with him, helping look after his girls. He also warned me not to do anything with his girls. I thought, '*No way, I knew he would kill me.*'

My job working with Fred was to pick up the girls and take them home. I also did security for the girls. I'd sit in the staff room waiting for the emergency buzzer to go off, which was there if the girls got into trouble with any clients. All the girls had to do was ring the buzzer, and myself and another guy would go into the room and bash the person and then throw them out, which happened often.

It was interesting just sitting and talking to the girls, finding out about why they were doing this line of work. They had some interesting stories. So many that I could probably write a book about what goes on in that industry.

The Crew

So, I looked after the escort girls for a couple of years, and eventually, I left as I had other things to do.

The crew of mates I grew up with, started to get organised with their criminal activities. One of them named Ray, who was a couple of years younger than me was always doing some wild things, very daring. For instance, one day he and a few others went to a bikie gang's clubhouse, they walked in with guns and held them up. They stole their drugs and cash and took off.

But there was a comeback, the bikies hunted them down and nearly killed them. They got off lightly, but Ray didn't stop there, he robbed a warehouse and shot a night patrol guy. When he went to court, he got off because he had one of the best lawyers in Melbourne. He was using heroin and had to go to drug rehabilitation.

The next time I saw him, he invited me to this boathouse that he'd bought. He had started a crew with a lot of guys who went to our school as well as guys from the streets. Their ages varied from about ten years older than us, to guys who were five or so years younger. Well, Ray straight up was leader, and no one challenged him. I thought the older guys might have, but they were followers and listened to him.

When the crew began, Ray was in charge, and some of the older guys became his right-hand men, they were in charge of the rest of us. He had a few guys setting up hydroponic weed growing in their houses for him. Ray even had linesmen in his pocket who jumped the power for him. The crop would be set up, and it would grow and be well nurtured.

When it was time to harvest the crop, he would take the largest share, and we would get what was left. We had no problems with getting busted. Ray had a few coppers on his books who would help to protect what was growing. He had the other crew members, including me, who helped to sell it on the streets. You would have people who would pick up a pound or so, and when they didn't come up with the cash, Ray would send crew members around to collect. If you didn't have the cash, you would lose your car or furniture, plus pay interest on top of what you owed.

Ray's business was booming; if someone told us that they had bought pot from another dealer who was growing; the grower would get a visit by the guys and would be shut down. Many growers would say, "Fuck off, who the fuck are you?" Ray would turn up the heat, and they were made to do things his way or lose everything as well as get a good bashing. He would fuck up your life, so in the end, they would always do things his way.

But, they were offered a role in growing on a bigger scale with Ray's protection. He would have a person call around and check on how the plants were growing and give the advice to get the best results. When it was ready to harvest, you would get your money, and he would get his. All over the Western suburbs, he had many set-ups with the money coming in.

After the club had been done up, it was terrific. It had a fully stocked bar, Foxtel and a pool table. I would see bundles of cash coming in and taken into Ray's little office. Some days there would be two or three guys spending hours in there just counting the cash. I knew he had this well under control, and I felt that I was a big part of something.

Months went by, and things did change for me. I wasn't always there as I was supposed to be. I guess I liked doing all sorts of other stuff with other people plus I liked travelling and would take off at times to visit Mum in Queensland or over to South Australia to see my cousin.

The Crew

Things were going great, plenty of money was coming in, and I was carrying around two wallets full of cash. I spent it on records, cars and gambling. Once, Ray asked me to go into Footscray to do a collection on some druggie who owed him three thousand dollars for some drugs he bought on credit. He told me to go there and bring back the money or something to that value. I said, "Okay," and headed off.

It was a high-rise housing commission flat, around twelve stories high. There always seemed to be more crime in the lower-income area. Stepping into the elevator, I went up about eight floors and found the door that I was meant to be at and knocked on it.

A voice replied, "Yes, who is it?" "Open up!" I said.

A pretty girl came to the door; she was thin and looked spaced out. She said, "Who are you?" I said, "I am here to collect some cash you owe Ray."

She looked at me and said, "I don't know anything about that." I walked passed her, and her boyfriend was sitting on the lounge. He looked stoned, but not on pot more like heroin.

He was a real skinny, dirty looking runt. I looked around, but there was nothing of value in the place, so I stood in front of him and said, "Have you got the cash for Ray?"

He said, "No, sorry, I need a couple of more days."

"No, I have to go back with something. If you don't have the cash, do you have a car or something worth the value, so that I can give you a couple more days?" I told him.

His reply was nasty. "Who are you? Fuck off!" He said. At that point, I grabbed him, opened the window and shoved the top half of his body out saying, "You're going to fly to the bottom if you don't pay now!"

His girlfriend started yelling "Stop! Don't hurt him, I'll do anything you want, let me help, but just don't hurt him?"

I looked at her and thought to myself *'She is nice looking and got the body.'* I said, "Okay, well you are coming with me, and you can work the bill off."

She replied, "Yes, okay, anything."

So, I grabbed her by the wrist and said, "Come with me." I turned to the boyfriend and told him: "If you want to see her again you'd better come up with that three thousand dollars."

He answered, "I will, I will."

She came with me, hopped into the car, and we went back to the club. Ray looked at me and asked, "Have you got the cash?"

I said, "He didn't have it and had nothing of value worth the debt, but I have his girlfriend." He looked at her, looked at me, laughed and said, "You're unreal, Mick."

I said, "What do you mean?"

He said, "I've never dealt in human trade, but fair enough. Can you pour a beer?" Ray asked her. She said, "Yes."

Ray said, "Well, take your clothes off, just leave on your panties and get behind the bar." So she did.

She started working off the debt. After a few days, I found out she wasn't just pouring beers. If someone wanted to fuck her, Ray would tell her to go into the bedroom that was there and fuck this guy, give him what he wanted and then get back to the bar. Of course, he was the one getting the money for her service. I felt a bit sorry for her and thought *'What have I done?'* A week later, Ray asked me to go and see if that 'worm' had his money. I thought, '*If he pays, his girlfriend will be free to go.*'

I headed back to those flats and knocked on the door. There was no answer. One of the neighbours came out and asked if I was looking for the people who lived there. They said that no one lived there anymore. About two days ago the police were there because the man in there had overdosed on drugs and they had found him dead. I thanked the lady for the information. I thought, '*Wow.*'

I went back to the club and said to Ray, "Sorry, the guy is dead, and there is no money." He looked at me and said, "Well, she's paid his debt, get her out of here."

I was like okay. I told her, "You're free to go home, the debt is paid. I will drive you home."

Heading to the car, I wondered how I was going to tell her about her boyfriend. Halfway there, I said, "I have got something to tell you. Your boyfriend is dead."

She was screaming at me saying, "You killed him!"

I said, "No, he overdosed."

She yelled out, "No! You're lying"

I told her I wasn't. I pulled up and said to her that I would walk her to her flat. But she still didn't believe me, and she still thought he would be there. She opened the door screaming out his name, but there was no answer. At this point, she didn't want me to stay and told me to leave.

On my way home, I thought about her and even after a couple of days, still feeling bad. I would check on her to see if she needed anything. I headed over to her place, went up in the elevator and knocked on the door; there was no answer.

I turned to see the neighbour again; she came out crying, asking me, "Are you looking for the girl?"

I said, "Yes, why are you crying?"

She looked at me and said, "It's so terrible the police were here yesterday again, that poor girl threw herself out the window because she couldn't cope without her boyfriend."

I thought to myself, *'Oh my god,'* and I then said, "Okay, thank you, bye."

Back at the club still in shock, Ray looked at me and said, "Looks like you have seen a ghost Mick, what's up?"

I said, "That girl."

"What girl?" He asked.

"The girl who worked here, she jumped out the window, she's dead."

He looked at me and said, "Stupid junkies."

I thought, *'No one cares.'* I turned around and said to Ray, "Well in the future, I'm not collecting money for you, find someone else and give me a new job."

He looked at me and said, "Yeah no problems." He then walked away. I felt for years that somehow it was all my fault that two people had died.

My new job was learning about hydroponic growing. It was the latest growing method. I watched and learned. I helped set up a few places around the suburbs, and once they were set up, I would call around to check and see how it was going or help until they were ready to harvest.

Once harvested and divided, the grower got forty per cent, and sixty per cent went to Ray. He had police in his pocket, who would also get a cut. The police knew which houses to raid and which ones not to raid that was Ray's. Ray knew how to jump the power as well, so the houses wouldn't have an enormous power bill, this was saving him loads of cash at this time.

Ray had about a dozen set-ups around the western suburbs. Years later he ended up having close to a hundred houses growing, so big money was moving through the club, and a lot of members had their work cut out making sure he wasn't getting ripped off. If a new grower started up a hydro set-up, when Ray found out about it, he would send a couple of lads around to make an offer which would either be, you shut down or join him, or you'd go on a holiday.

He would send a guy around to help fix your set-up and improve on it to make it bigger and better and protected from the law. The grower would end up with forty per cent of what they grew, and Ray took sixty per cent, which was a pretty good offer.

Ray would win because he didn't have to go anywhere near the place and would be making shit loads of cash. Out of his cut, he would be paying the boys for keeping things running and of course, the cops to work with him. Things ran smoothly before pills 'ice' came onto the streets. I knew a couple of the cops that he had on his payroll; they were assholes. As kids, we would have run-ins with them at times.

One night I was walking down the street. I was about sixteen years old and had an ounce of hash on me. I was going to a place to slice it up to sell, but this cop, I won't say his name, pulled up and said, "Mick, where are you going?"

I said, "Just home."

He said, "Empty your pockets." So I did. He then said, "What's in the bag?"

I had the bag hung over my shoulder. I said, "Nothing."

"Well, give me a look," he said.

Of course, the ounce was in the bag, he saw it there and said, "What do we have here?" He took the bag and put it in his car and then said, "Well, it's your lucky day; you can now fuck off." What could I do? So, I moved on. I was so pissed off at him because I was down three hundred dollars, but I suppose it's better than being charged. That was the kind of thing he would do.

There was a pizza shop in Newport with pool tables out the back. There was a door at the end of this room. Behind that door, there would be Italians playing cards. They were playing for big money.

This cop would walk into the pizza shop order a pizza which he wouldn't pay for and walk past us boys saying, "G' day lads." Then he would walk straight into that room and ask for his envelope that had cash in it. He would then turn a blind eye to their gambling. The Italians hated doing it, but it kept the peace.

Years later, as Ray's business grew more significant with the crew, this cop was the first person he had in his pocket. The cop then became a detective, and this was even better for Ray as he received inside information from him. I could see where things were going and thought, '*Good for him.*' But at the same time, I didn't like the way things were. People were getting hurt along the way. I guess deep down I knew I wasn't like that, but I had to show a tougher side to me to put fear into people.

One day I ran into a mate that I had known for years. I went to school with him. His name was Danny. He was now using heavier drugs like coke and heroin. I felt sorry for him because at school we were close and I had seen the nice side to him, but as drugs do, they change nice people into monsters.

Anyway, he said, "How you been Mick?"

I said, "Yeah good, but I am getting a bit sick of everything here, I wouldn't mind a change. I'm thinking of heading up to Queensland."

He said, "Well, let me know if you do because I would like to come with you and when we get up there, I will introduce you to people I know. They will get you some work."

I said, "Yeah, sure."

So, I went home and said to Sam, "Would you like to go back home to Queensland so you can be close to your family?"

She replied, "Fuck yeah, I hate it here." So, I said, "Okay, we will go."

Chapter 14

TINS OF HEROIN

Within the next few weeks, we had packed up and moved up to Queensland. Danny contacted me and said he would be in touch and was coming up in a few weeks. I thought no more about it. We arrived at mum's house. We asked if we could stay for a month or so until we got our place. Mum was happy for us to stay, especially as she was seeing April, her granddaughter. Within a month we got a house at Clontarf, a coastal suburb, it's about thirty kilometres out of Brisbane, it was a nice area to live.

A few weeks of settling into the new house, we had bought new furniture etc. I received a call from Danny. "G'day Mick, I'm at the airport, can you come to get me?"

"Sure," I said. I headed off to the airport. As I saw him walking towards me, I thought, *'Cool, a mate from Melbourne is up here. I don't know anyone up here, so it will be good to see an old mate.'*

It wasn't long after we arrived at my home that I could see from Sam's face that she wasn't impressed, thinking, *'Great one of your criminal mates is here now.'* I didn't take much notice as we didn't have a healthy relationship. We were only staying together for April's sake. Later in life, I realised you shouldn't live like that.

Tins of Heroin

After Danny arrived, he said to me, "Tomorrow can we go into the Valley?" The Valley was in the city; it is a part of Brisbane that has a lot of colourful people, like prostitutes, drug addicts, scammers, dealers and dirty streets.

Chinatown was in the same area. Like any city that has a Chinatown, you would know what I mean, lots of Chinese restaurants and shops etc. So, I was happy to take Danny but asked him why we were going there.

Danny replied, "I want you to meet a friend of mine who owns a business; they will give you a job."

I said, "Great, doing what?"

He said it would be driving.

I was thinking, '*Okay, let's go!*'

We drove into the Valley and entered a warehouse where a few Chinese people were working, packing boxes. On entering the office area, a lady at the counter told us to take a seat. We sat down, and I started looking around the room, through a door came these two Chinese men.

One was a well-dressed businessman, and the other was in a suit, a scruffy-looking big guy, I wouldn't even think of messing with him. Danny said, "Hi, this is my mate Mick who I was telling you about," as he introduced me to them. I don't remember their names; they came in, sat down and had a coffee with us.

The well-dressed guy said, "Danny tells me you want some work." I eagerly agreed. "Do you have your license?" He asked.

I said, "Yes."

"Okay, You would be doing some driving jobs for me, in a small truck that you can drive with your car license. You'll be delivering our products to all the Chinese restaurants down the Gold Coast, out west, up to the north coast and around Brisbane. You okay with that?" He said. I said, "Sure." I thought, *'Great, an honest job.'*

Living up here was starting to look good, and I thought *'Here's a chance to change my life.'* Well, I was later to find out I was wrong; I was unaware that I was getting myself deeper into trouble.

I turned up to start work, and they welcomed me. There was this Chinese guy, the one that looked like a shifty type of guy; he was wearing a brown suit that looked like it needed to be at the dry cleaners. There were cigarette marks and wine stains over it. He came out to me with a smoke hanging out of his mouth and said, "You go with this guy; he will teach you everything."

"Okay," I said.

The guy walked over and said, "Hi, I am Tonga." He was well-built about my age, twenty-one, he was a nice guy. He told me he grew up in Papua New Guinea and told stories about how his grandfather used to headhunt other tribes. I was interested and shocked at what he told me.

We climbed into the truck and started doing deliveries down the Gold Coast. About two weeks on the job, the boss came and told me that I would be doing this run on my own now that Tonga was doing another run. I said, "Okay, no problems." I was going to start the next day, and I was okay with it as I knew my way around.

Things were going well, one day the suited guy said to me "See this box, you put it in the cab of the truck, and when you get to the restaurant you give this box to him and collect a red envelope."

I said, "Sure, no problems."

Tins of Heroin

Heading towards the restaurant, I looked at the box with oyster sauce written on it. It contained cans. I thought, *'I loaded the other oyster sauce boxes on the truck, why is this one special?'* I followed the orders though; I gave the box to this Chinese man who came out of the kitchen from around the back.

He looked like he was a hundred years old; he was a little guy with a smoke hanging out of his mouth. He started yelling, "You come in, you come this way." He told me to sit down and asked if I wanted anything to eat.

I said, "Anything." He handed the box to a younger guy who walked away with it.

The old Chinese guy, with the smoke hanging out of his mouth started cooking me some lemon chicken and fried rice. He said, "Now you eat." By the time I was finished eating in the kitchen, the guy who took the box had come back out with a red envelope and said, "You take this." I thanked them. I hopped back into the truck and drove to my next drop. As I was driving, I was thinking, *'There was something dodgy about this.'* But thought no more about it.

Arriving back to the depot about 5 p.m., I said to the suited guy, "Here is your envelope." He opened it in front of me, it contained hundred dollar bills, probably three inches thick. He takes one out and hands it to me and said, "You've done well." I took the money, said thanks and walked away.

About two weeks later, the same thing happened again, another hundred dollars for me. I said nothing, but I couldn't help wondering what was going on because this went on for months. I started taking three or four boxes down to different restaurants. Danny turned up one day driving an old white XA Ford panel van.

I walked over and said, "Hey Danny, how have you been? What brings you back to Queensland?"

He looked wired like he was on something and replied, "Yeah, I drove up from Melbourne through the night, so I'm a bit buggered, I took something to keep me going."

"How long do you think you are staying?" I asked.

"Well, for a few days, we'll go out while I'm here," he replied.

"Great," I said.

He headed into the office, and ten minutes later, he came out with the Chinese boss, they headed out to the van where I saw them taking out boxes with oyster sauce written on them. I kept loading my truck, and when I was ready to head off, I yelled to Danny, "See you later." He waved and said, "Sure, tonight." And off I went down to the Gold Coast to do my deliveries.

Later that night I arrived home, and my daughter April was happy to see me, she was crawling around the floor and her mum, Sam was cooking dinner.

The phone rang, it was Danny. "Hi Mick, what are you doing?" He said.

I said, "About to have dinner, come over if you like."

He said, "No, I'm down the Gold Coast at the casino. Why don't you come down?"

So I said, "Yeah okay, I will see you there." I turned to Sam and said, "I won't be staying for dinner. I'm going to the casino."

She turned and said, "Whatever."

Things weren't that good between us, we were doing our own thing, we just had a child together, and that's all it was, we had no love for each other." I guess she was right;

we were too young to know what to do. I just stayed for April's sake, which a lot of people do when they have kids, and they try and stay together.

After getting changed, I jumped in my car which at the time was a nice blue VE Valiant, with the pinstripes down the sides, hot wire mags, a sporty car. I drove down the coast and walked into the casino looking for Danny.

Mobile phones weren't around then, so you couldn't just ring or text to find someone. I headed to the bar, that's where he normally would be, and sure enough, he was sitting there drinking and talking to a nice looking blonde girl about twenty years old. She wore a dark green evening dress, and she had a great smile.

Danny turned and saw me saying, "Hey, Mick, you made it!"

I said, "Yeah, what do you want me to do?"

"Well, a bit of gaming and bit of business." He said.

"Cool," I said.

We headed over to the two-up rings where you toss two coins and choose heads or tails. I gave this a go, and two or three hours later, I am up to two thousand dollars. I thought *'This is good, it's a rush.'* Every week for months, I kept going back, then one day I just stopped; I had so much other shit I had to do. I was too busy.

After winning that night, I asked him, "Danny, what's up for the rest of the night?" He said, "Well I am heading up to my room in the casino. So Mick, go and grab a feed and kill a couple more hours, then come up to my room." He gave me the number, and I said, "Yeah cool." He was heading up to the room with this blonde that he had picked up, and I went looking for a feed.

After I finished eating, I realised that I have never played roulette, so I thought I would give it a go. About an hour later I'd won another fifteen hundred dollars, thinking, *'This is my lucky night.'* I headed up to Danny's room, finding his room number, I knocked on the door, and Danny yelled: "Who is it?"

"It's me, Mick," I said.

"Yeah mate, open the door," he said.

I walked in, and he is laying on the bed, drinking a beer, and the girl was in the bathroom. He said, "Grab a seat, mate. Do you like your job?"

I said, "Yeah, good; I'm enjoying it."

"Is the boss looking after you?" He asked.

I said, "Yeah but seems some days I take those boxes you had in your van down the coast, once or twice a week, and when I get back, he swings me an extra hundred dollars cash in my hand, which is good on top of my pay."

Danny looked at me with a grin and said, "That's good, mate. Do you know what you're carrying in those boxes?"

"I feel something is suspicious, but hey Danny I wouldn't ask that Chinese fella, he is a scary bloke," I said.

Danny replied, "Mick, I will tell you something but keep this to yourself."

I thought to myself, *'Okay, I'm listening!'*

He said, "Well I've got a connection in Melbourne on the docks. When a container comes in, it's an order for a Chinese restaurant owner in Melbourne. He is a very powerful businessman; he gets heroin brought in inside those cans. My job is to make sure the customs guy, who we have on our books, working at the docks lets me know when it has arrived. He opened the container for me, and

Tins of Heroin

we loaded it onto a truck and took the boxes to a warehouse where we collect the boxes which contain the heroin.

All of the officials get paid to turn their heads; I pick up a load of boxes and bring them up here, and they drop them off when you deliver your loads of rice and soy sauce to the restaurants down here. Certain people buy these boxes and sell it on the streets. I said, "I thought something was fishy.

"Well, you have told me enough, Danny, but I didn't know if I wanted to know all of this information. What if one day I get pulled up and get caught?" I would go down, but then thought, *'What are the chances of that happening?'* I didn't worry about it after that. We drank some more, and I crashed out.

The next morning, I got up and told Danny, who was still in bed with the girl, that I was leaving and would see him next time. I was wondering what Danny had got himself into, as I headed home going over what he had told me.

About a year later that Danny told me that it had come back to bite him in the ass. I was home; I put the cash I had won on the kitchen table and headed to bed. I was so tired. Sam was at her mum's with April. I thought, *'Great, some more sleep and I will be fine.'*

A few hours went by until I woke up and walked out to the kitchen and noticed my cash was gone, I thought, *'What the hell?'* I noticed that Sam had been home, so I thought maybe she had put the money somewhere safer.

It was Saturday, I had a shower and got ready to go into town for a feed. I headed into town, and when I got back a couple of hours later, Sam was home. Entering the house, she happily asked if I had a win at the casino last night.

I replied, "Yeah, where's my money?"

She said, "I went to the shops and bought a few things."

I said, "Okay, what?"

"Well, I bought a microwave, some make-up, a new fridge and clothes for April," Sam said.

I thought, *'That's okay, but you could have woken me and told me what you were going to do.'*

I thought to myself, *'What a bitch for just taking and spending it.' 'Oh well.'* I thought, *'It's all good, I'll just go down again in a couple of days and win some more,'* which I ended up doing. I took five hundred dollars down with me and lost the lot that hurt. But the next few times I went, I did win a few thousand, so I found myself a new hobby, but that could be a bad thing too.

The business was booming when I returned to work; it was coming into February when they celebrate it was Chinese New Year. The boss was putting on a party in Chinatown in the Valley at a restaurant. He told us to bring our partner, so I did.

We arrived at the restaurant, beautifully decorated and I noticed the other workers were there. Chico, one of the first people I met when I started, was there with his girlfriend. We sat at a large table which seated about eight people, and there were about six of these tables, all of them occupied with workers, office staff and the bosses.

In the middle of each table, they had a lazy Susan, which is a mini-table which can spin around stacked with food which we shared and consumed throughout the night. Chinese dragons danced throughout the restaurant, which I had never seen before; they were amazing.

Later that night as I was leaving, the boss came up to me, you could tell he was a bit drunk, he walked over and said "Michael, this is for you, I appreciate the work you have been doing for me." It was a red envelope. He said, "Red is good luck for Chinese."

I said, "Thank you." I shook his hand and said, "Great night, I've got to go."

"No worries, thank you," he said.

Heading out to my car, Sam asked, "What is in the envelope?" I opened it, and it had five hundred dollars in it.

Well, I thought, *'They're happy with me, and this is what they do for their workers,'* but I found out later, the other workers only received one hundred dollars in their envelopes. But they weren't doing what I was for them, which was delivering their boxes to the Gold Coast.

They thought I didn't know, Danny had told me, but I always acted as if I was driving a delivery truck and knew nothing.

One night I was driving home from the Gold Coast, and it was about 6 o'clock, and sometimes it was easier to take the truck home when it was late. It saved going into the city. I could go straight up to Redcliffe where I lived, much easier I thought.

This night I was a block or so from home when a cop car pulled me over. "What's in the truck?" He asked.

"Just a few things extra after my deliveries; like a bag of rice and a few boxes." I replied. I always had a little extra on board just in case an order was short.

The cop asked, "Can I have a look at your license?" I handed it to him. He came back from his car and said, "Give me a look in the back." He checked the back of the truck and then looked at his partner and said, "I'm giving you a ticket." I asked what I did wrong.

He said, "For going through a stop sign."

I replied, "That's bullshit; I never did!"

He said, "Do you want to come down to the station?"

I said, "No, and you can stick your ticket."

He then said, "Come with us; lock your truck."

Well, I did just that and went with them in the cop car back to the station.

At that time, I didn't know much about the law. So I obeyed. On my way there, I thought, *'It was a bit odd that they are taking me to the station over a supposed stop sign infringement.'* At the station, they took me to a room and told me to sit there and that a detective would come to talk to me soon. Sitting there thinking, *'What the hell?'*

Suddenly two detectives came in. One was fat and untidy wearing a brown suit with his shirt hanging out; he had grey hair, going bald with a nasty look on his face. The other one was a thin, clean, younger-looking guy wearing a dark blue suit. He was the first person to speak. "Hello, I'm Detective Dan Smith. We have something we want to show you," he pulled out a clear bag with white powder in it and said, "What do you know about this?"

I replied, "What! I have never seen this before; I don't even know what it is?"

Even though I was sure it was heroin, I acted dumb but also surprised. The fat cop said, "Well we know you work for the Chinese in the Valley, and we also know that they're moving this stuff down the coast, and you are their delivery driver."

I replied, "I only deliver their rice and supplies to their restaurants; I have never seen this stuff before." I was starting to get a bit worried.

"Look, you can tell us what you know, and we will let you go, and you can forget about the stop sign fine," he said.

I said, "I can't tell you anything."

They said, "Do you know a Danny blah, blah?" I started to realise what was happening; they must have busted Danny.

I said, "Danny, who? Don't know him."

"Well he knows you and going by what he is telling us, you do know him. He tells us you are a driver for them." He said.

I said, "Maybe he has seen me there, but I don't know him, okay!"

The fat cop said, "You can go, but you will be hearing from us again soon."

I left there thinking *'What the hell, Danny must be in there, and maybe they have got him for the gear somehow, and he has flipped and has told them everything.'* I didn't know what to think. I went home feeling a bit light-headed wondering what was going to happen. When I went into work the next day, I played it by ear and acted cool. I followed my usual routine, loading my truck and carried on as though nothing had happened.

A few days went by. I was leaving home for work and got around the corner, and these two cops pulled me over. "Hello, how are you? Where are you off to?" One of them said.

"I'm going to work," I replied.

"Well, your brake light isn't working," the cop said.

I said, "Really! I didn't realise that." I got out, had a look and said, "It is working fine."

He said, "No, it's not!" He proceeded to smash it with his torch.

I looked and thought, *'Can they do that? What's going on?'* I thought, *'Here you go, there's a fine for that.'*

A few days later, another fine for speeding came, I wasn't even speeding. As they didn't have speed cameras in those days; it was their word against yours. It was the same cop in the space of two months, and I received about fifteen tickets for all sorts of other things.

One day I heard my dog barking out the front. It was the same two detectives coming to visit me. I asked, "What do you want now?"

They said, "I hear you have been getting a few fines lately. Would you like them to disappear? We can do that. All you need to do is tell us everything you know about what is going on at work, and we can protect you."

I replied, "Piss off! I don't know anything." They took off.

The next day I went into work and quit. I told the boss I was moving back to Melbourne. The truth was: I had had enough of these cops and thought *'It's only a matter of time before they pulled me over in my truck when I have these boxes on board. I'll cop it for sure then, with carrying heroin, fuck that.'* So it was easier to quit.

A few months later, another mate of mine, Andrew arrived up from Melbourne to visit me: He too was on the gear and asked to stay with us for a while. I didn't mind as someone from home made me feel good, and it was comfortable talking about stuff that was going on.

What a bad mistake that turned out to be. Andrew and I went to primary school together. He was a slim, good-looking guy, always well-dressed, and was a charmer with the girls. He had straight blonde hair and tan with professionally done tattoos on his arms.

Tins of Heroin

His mother had always spoiled him. He always had the newest dirt bikes and surf gear, best cricket bat, in the neighbourhood, while most of us kids had cheap stuff, homemade put-together bikes and second-hand things.

He was always getting into trouble, though. I couldn't understand why, even though he had the best of everything. He found it hard to fit in with the rest of us.

He turned up at my place because he had to get away from Melbourne. He said everyone was on the gear and he needed a new place to go to get away from it all. I said okay, and Sam didn't mind or didn't care. She was doing her own thing, working in the city washing cars in a car yard. We hardly spoke anyway. She had said 'Whatever.'

Andrew and I would go to the pub for a counter lunch and a few beers every day and go for a swim at the beach. We would chill until I had to go pick April up from kindergarten. I was getting bored, not working. Andrew was using drugs each day and asked me if I wanted to have some.

So I tried some speed, and when it hit me, it gave me too much energy and kept me awake for two days. It drove me mad unless I was doing something. I would clean the house and then do it again ten minutes later. I felt like I could get fit on this. So the next day, I asked: "Andrew, do you have any more of this?"

"Yeah, here you go," he said.

Taking these drugs started another problem. As each day went by, I wanted more, but it cost so much.

Andrew told me he had an idea. I asked, "What is it?"

He replied, "Well up here in Queensland; things are a lot different compared to Melbourne."

I said, "Yeah, I know that a lot of things are, but what are you talking about?"

He said, "Well if you go to a real estate tell them you want to rent a place, you ask if you can take a look at the property and they hand you the keys. They tell you to go have a look and if you like it, come back to fill out an application form."

I replied, "Yeah, I know."

Andrew said, "Well, in Melbourne, how do they do it?"

"They take you to the property or meet you there," I said.

"See," he said.

I thought, *"See what?"*

Andrew said, "Well, up here you get the keys and go take a look. But you don't look at the property. You get the key cut, keep it and go back to the real estate and give back their keys."

"So now we have a key to a place, so what now?" I said.

"Well what you do is go to a few real estates, but not just in Redcliffe but other suburbs, do the same thing, and once you have twenty or thirty keys, we tag them to let us know which house is for what key.

Later we would go back after people have moved in and while they are at work, we come along, walk straight in, spend ten minutes in and get what we can and get out. We can do this to each house that we have a key. We can do it again in a new area with different houses." He said.

I thought, *'I'm not that kind of person. Andrew makes it sound easy, though I don't know.'*

Chapter 15

BOGGO ROAD

After a day of thinking about it, Andrew kept trying to sell me the idea.

He said, "Well, let's try just a couple and see how we go." I thought, *'Okay, just a couple won't hurt.'*

So the next day off we went looking at rentals and going into real estate offices asking for keys to look at properties. We went into a shopping centre and found a guy that cut keys. We got three keys cut for three different houses. So far, so good.

We went to the pub, and while we were there, I was thinking about what we had done. Andrew said, "Well, all we do now is wait a week or so, then we hit those houses."

I said, "What do we take?"

He said, "Jewellery, whatever we can sell."

'Okay,' I thought.

About two weeks went by, and now we hit the first house. We grabbed a few items and went to a guy's place, and he bought the stuff off us. We only got about two hundred dollars, which I thought wasn't worth it. Plus I didn't feel good about myself doing it. I would do one more, and then I would stop this.

We robbed the next house the following day, and oh my god, there were guns in the wardrobe and jewellery, which got me excited. Andrew said he knew someone in the city that we could unload the guns to, so off we went. We thought we would make a couple of grand, but even if we did, I'm stopping because I didn't like this.

We went to the city to meet this guy, but unbeknown to us, the cops were monitoring him. We got out of the car and this older guy, probably in his thirties, came walking over. Andrew knew him, so they were talking, he looked suspicious to me, but I thought as long as he buys the stuff, that's all that matters.

We opened the boot of the car to show this guy, and suddenly, I hear these voices, "Freeze! Put your hands on the roof of the car, get over here," said the detectives as they grabbed me. "What you got in the boot, who owns this stuff?" *'Great,'* I thought.

I didn't speak, first rule. "Well, you guys are coming with us in the cop car!" We climbed into an unmarked XE Falcon, drove to the nearest cop station, where we sat for about two hours and questioned. They said, "You live in Redcliffe, and that is where the guns came from, so you two are going there."

Off we go again about a forty-five-minute drive to Redcliffe cop station. I received the worst treatment of my life. It started with, 'Where did you get this stuff?" One cop had this file on him that was about an inch thick, and he said: "See this, there are about fifty robberies in this file, and you're going to cop most of them." I thought, *'Fuck that!'*

They separated us into rooms down the hall from each other. The two cops told us each to take a seat. I sat down on this office chair that had wheels on it.

Then one copper said, "Put your hands behind the seat." He handcuffed me. "Tell us how many of these places you have robbed," he said.

I said, "None." He punched me in my chest, and the chair went across the room to where the other cop was waiting who punched me again in my shoulder.

The police continued this treatment for about an hour until they left the room. I thought this is fucked, and I was feeling sore; it was painful. After fifteen minutes or so, they came back into the room and said, "Are you going to tell us anything?" I said nothing. I wasn't telling them anything.

They grabbed me and put me into a locker, one of those you put your stuff in at a workplace, tall narrow and made of some metal. Once inside the locker, the detectives were hitting something against it like a torch, something hard. They kept banging all over the locker. The noise was deafening, and it could drive you insane. I felt them pick up the locker with a trolley, and I was getting wheeled somewhere.

Next thing I know, I was flying upside down and sideways, they had tipped it down the stairwell in the fire escape of this two-story cop station. They were playing games with me. I was in shock thinking these fucking cops are fucked up. After they did that, they wheeled me back to the office, got me out of the locker and told me to sit down again into the chair.

I was in pain all over, and they started asking me, "What are you going to tell us?"

"Get fucked!" I said.

They left the room, and after twenty minutes passed nothing, I was sitting there thinking all sorts of things like if they come back and start hitting me again, I'm going to get up connected to this chair and jump straight through the glass window which was one floor up. I might land on the ground outside and break a few bones, but let's see them explain how and why that happened, this was the point I was at with these clowns.

Sitting there, all I could hear was Andrew in the other room, screaming. I couldn't imagine what they were doing to him? All of a sudden, it went quiet, about ten minutes later, two new detectives entered. "Well, your mate has told us everything and has written it down and signed it," they said.

I was thinking, *'Great.'* I replied, "I don't believe you."

"Well, you come with us," said one of the detectives.

They walked me down the hallway to the room where they were holding Andrew. In front of me, one of them said to him, "Did you sign this?"

He said, "Yes." I looked at him, his nose looked broken, and he was bloodied and beaten up.

I didn't say anything to him. I turned and walked away back to the room I was in before and sat down. I said, "Well, I'm not making any statement, you have his so you can do whatever turns you on, you cunts!" I thought, *'I'm going to cop it now.'*

They just walked out and came back ten minutes later and said, "Right you're going to be charged. Once we do that you're going to the watch-house until you get bail."

So, I am in a cell that seemed pretty clean. I was sitting there waiting. After an hour or so, I heard the cops processing Andrew first. I started yelling, "What about me?"

Someone yelled back, "You can wait!"

Another two hours went by, and Andrew is well and truly gone, I guess they thought since Andrew told them everything that I might go after him.

So, they had given him a good head start. After they processed me, I walked out. I was more upset with the way the cops treated me than Andrew. I went home and thought, *'Now what am I going to do?'* I never saw Andrew again. Oh well, my stupid fault for getting involved in it.

About a month later, I had to face court over these fines that I had been getting. I turned up at court, and the duty lawyer said to me, "Just pay them."

I said, "No way! I'll fight it." I went in to face the judge.

He asked me, "What are you going to do with these fines?"

I said, "Well, I'm not paying them. As you might notice, all of them have been given to me by the same cop. Don't you think that is suspicious?" I said.

He just looked at me and said: "Well, you have just been unlucky, so are going to pay them or not?"

I said, "Not." He gave me two months in jail instead. I could not believe my ears. I thought they were all corrupt up here. They took me to the watch-house; there was no going home.

I ended up at a jail called Boggo Road. It had two sections, the new building and the old building. The new one had all the modern stuff, your cell, a gym, an oval to walk around. It wasn't too bad. The old building was a hundred years old, it had nothing, and it was like going back in time. I started my time in the new section and got settled there.

It was an eye-opener, it was a lot different from a boy's home. I witnessed people stabbed, and the screws were nasty. I kept friends with a couple of guys playing chess and ball games, which was okay, and the food was good. I guess I'll do my time. After two weeks, I had to go to court again over the break and enters.

I left the jail in a prison van and was taken off to the watch-house, waiting to face court. My lawyer said because I was already in jail for the fines, that we would adjourn the case until I got out which would be in a few weeks.

The adjournment gave us extra time to prepare for the case. I was happy with that. So, it was time to head back to jail. I thought I was going back to the new jail, but someone had my room so I would have to go to the old jail for about a week.

There I would wait for a transfer to a minimum-security jail to finish my time. I thought, *'What a load of bullshit, all this over traffic fines.'* We arrived in the old section of the jail.

What a surprise that was. I felt like I went back in time a hundred years. The cells were dark. They only had a little window about the size of a porthole, and it smelled musty. There was no toilet in your room, just a bucket with a handle that you had to line up with each morning to empty.

After that, you would go to the food hall to sit and have your breakfast. You had to sit so close to someone that it was like you were on an old sailing ship elbow to elbow, no room at all. The food was crap.

After you ate, you would go out into a yard where all they had was four posts with an iron roof as your protection from the sun. If it rained from one direction, you would get soaked. There were two outside toilets, they had roof iron for walls, only three sides, no doors so people could walk past you watching you having a crap.

There was something they called the grey ghost. It was if someone wanted to bash you the grey ghost would appear. What it meant was is if you would be sitting on the loo having a crap and looked up and see a grey blanket coming towards you, that's all you would see.

It would be someone behind you who would throw it over and would hit you with anything available. It could be a weight bar or anything that would smash you up. They would then walk away, leaving you sitting on the loo, with your face smashed in and blood everywhere.

You would have no idea who it was as they were behind the grey blanket. Once the grey ghost had visited you, the screws would ask what happened, but you would have no idea. Lucky for me, I didn't see any ghost while having a crap. After a week went by I was released. I went back home and thought, *'Never again am I going back there.'* I started dwelling about this court case I was facing over the guns.

I went to see a lawyer. He said I would get about five years in jail at least. I thought, *'There is no way was I going back to jail.'* My relationship with Sam was not right, and I wasn't happy up here in Queensland. I thought it was best if I take off and go back to Melbourne and so that's what I did. I walked out on my daughter and Sam, and I caught a bus home. I arrived in Melbourne and turned up at a mate's place. His name was Warren.

Warren worked for the council as a gardener. He was a short, stocky, good-looking guy with a tan. Warren owned a blue Holden panel van with mags and bubble windows on the side of it; all decked out, a real show quality van. It was his pride and joy. He had a single bedroom flat across the road from the beach.

    His flat was all done up with palms and classy furniture. It looked like a resort. I asked if I could stay at his place for a week, and once I get work, I would move into a place of my own. He was okay with that. After a week went by, I could not find work. I thought that I couldn't stay here any longer. I felt I was in the way.

Chapter 16

MEETING DEB

Late one night I met this girl, her name was Debbie. She had big brown eyes and lovely long brown hair. She looked a little rough and had tattoos on her tits. Debbie was sitting having a coffee at this café. I went up and started to speak to her. We seemed to hit it off. I asked her what she was up to, and she said that she was heading to Adelaide in a couple of days.

I said, "Sounds cool."

"Where are you from?" She asked.

"Queensland, I just came down from there, and I'm staying at a mates place. I don't know what I'm doing at the moment." I said.

Debbie said, "Want to come to a party tonight at my girlfriend's?"

I said, "Sure, why not?"

We left the cafe and went for a walk along the beach. We hung out for too long; we held hands and had kissed.

I asked, "Would you like a joint?"

She said, "Fuck yeah!"

So I lit it up, we sat there not saying much, just watching the waves rolling in and chilling. A few hours went by, Debbie then said, "Let's get going to this party."

I said, "Yeah sure."

We walked to the party. It took about thirty minutes. Seemed more like two hours as we were both wasted. We finally arrived at the house. Debbie seemed only to know her friend, who was there and no one else, which was okay, so we separated and started to talk to others.

Noticing people coming and going from the bathroom; I thought I would look in there. As I opened the door, a voice said, "We're busy mate." I said, "It's okay, I'm cool with that." I walked in where they were taking lines of speed, I pulled out a joint and said, "Anyone want a toke?"

One girl said, "Cool, do you want a line?"

"Yeah, thanks," I said. So I had a line or two, maybe three. I came out of the bathroom, feeling alive with energy.

Looking around for Debbie, I saw her talking to her friend and said, "What are you doing later?"

"Nothing," she replied.

"Okay, let's bail soon, and I'll take you somewhere cool," I said.

"Okay," she said. I was buzzing and wanted fresh air. I needed to do something. After an hour went by we left.

Debbie asked, "What are we doing?"

I said, "Well, I'm going to steal a car, drive to my dealers' place, get some blow, and we'll go to the city to find my uncle."

"Okay, let's go," she said.

Just around the corner, we saw another party going on at this two-story place.

I said, "Let's gate crash here."

Deb said, "You sure?"

Meeting Deb

"Yeah, watch this, follow my lead," I told her. So, we went up to the door, opened it and walked in. The music was blaring, and there were lots of people there.

I went to the first person I saw and said: "How's it going?"

"Yeah good," he said.

"What's your name?" I asked.

He said, "Scott."

"Hi, I'm Mick, this is Deb," I said. We talked some shit for five minutes then I said to Deb, "Go talk to that girl over there; I will be with you soon."

I asked this Scott guy, "Any blow here?"

He said, "Yeah, go out back, look for this guy with the leather jacket he has some."

"Okay, cool," I said.

It was a beautiful house, old but well-kept, it had a lot of paintings on the walls and looked like a school teacher owned it, someone important who had money. So, I headed out the back of the house. I found the guy with the leather jacket. He was skinny, short dark hair, and he looked like he was shady.

I walked over and said, "G'day mate, I'm a friend of Scott's. He said you could help me with some blow."

"Yeah sure, just meet me in the bathroom inside in five okay," he said.

While I was walking back inside to look for Deb, this guy approached me, he was tall and fat with glasses, and I'm guessing he was the host.

"Hello, who are you?" He asked.

I replied, "Well, who are you?"

"I live here," he said.

I said, "Cool, I am a friend of Scott's."

"Okay, I guess you are okay then," he said.

"Yeah mate, I have known Scott for a while. We can go and get a feed if you like?" He said.

"I'm not feeling hungry," I said.

"But you might later," he said.

I headed back inside to find the bathroom. I saw Deb talking to the wife of the house. Everything looked okay.

The bathroom wasn't hard to find; it had a line up outside. I started talking to people. There were about four people in there having lines.

The guy with the leather jacket entered saying, "Okay, how much you after?"

I said, "A hundred dollars' worth."

"No problems," he said.

He pulled out a large bag and weighed it up for me.

"There you go, have a line and tell me what you think," he said.

So I did, and it blew me away. I said, "Thanks, mate, it's great."

Making my way to the kitchen, I noticed there were all these car keys sitting on the kitchen bench. I saw one set with a Porsche key ring. I grabbed it and went over to Deb.

In a soft voice, I said, "Meet me out the front in two minutes. That way, no one will think we are leaving together and get in our way or try to stop us."

She said, "Yeah okay." I headed out the front, and there were a few cars lined up the street.

Meeting Deb

There it was, a red Porsche. I felt a big rush as I walked over to it and opened the door. '*Unreal.*' I thought, as I jumped in and started it up. Out came Deb.

She hopped in and said, "You're not the only naughty one."

As we drove off, she pulled some jewellery out of her bra and said, "While you were scoring, I went upstairs and went through the woman's drawers in her bedroom and found these." There were some rings, a watch, and a couple of necklaces.

"Are you going to keep them?" I asked.

"No, I don't want them, I was hoping you could sell them?"

"Yeah, no problems, we'll head to St. Kilda and see my uncle, he owns a strip club and escort business. He will give me something for them."

So we drove to my Uncle Fred's place. We pulled up around the corner from his house.

"We will park here so if the cops see this car it's not in front of my Uncle's place. He would kill me if I brought that kind of attention to him. Use your shirt or something to wipe any prints off it."

"Okay," she said.

We hopped out and started to walk to Fred's, which was about five minutes away. When we arrived, there was a guy out the front. I knew him; he was a massive guy dressed well, standing at the door to keep out people that aren't good enough to be going in.

I said, "G'day, how are you? Is my Uncle Fred in tonight?"

"Yeah Mick, just go upstairs, he's up there."

We both headed in, and Deb's eyes lit up as she had never been in a place like this. Girls were walking around in G-strings, all done up, waiting on guys for drinks and music and rooms with some nice dim lights in them.

I said, "You wait here with the girls."

I introduced her to one, I knew and said, "Can you look after Deb while I go upstairs?"

This girls name was Roxy, well that was her show name. I don't know what her real name was. She was about twenty-two with red hair and a great body.

She said, "No problems, Mick. Could I see you for a minute when you get back?"

I said, "Okay," and headed upstairs.

Knocking on the door, I heard his voice, "Yeah, it's Mick, Uncle Fred."

"Yeah, come in," he said. I walked into the room and saw there were two girls in there. He had a lounge and coffee table with a large crystal ashtray in the centre, some boxing pictures on the walls, a large mirror on another wall and bottles of whiskey on his desk.

He stood up, walked around his desk and said, "What the fuck have you been up to?"

I said, "Not much. I haven't got a place to live, so I'm just wandering around. I might head over to Adelaide and see what's there."

"Nothing over there, Mick. Last time I was there I stayed in a nasty jail called Yalta, you don't want to visit that place," he said.

Fred always went on about jails and cops. He hated them as he had spent a lot of his youth in and out of prisons. He'd been in Sydney jail as well, and he got to know some nasty people. I met some of these people by just being with him.

Some of these people I met carried handguns and weren't very social. I always felt a little scared over the years. Fred would have done all sorts of jobs with them. Such as safes, trucks, factory jobs, cars, shops whatever had value in them, he also did the odd bashing.

Fred had done some hard time, and it had done some damage to him. He would go a bit nuts at times when he drank. I felt uncomfortable around him, but tonight, he was not drunk and was in a good mood. "I was hoping you could help me, Uncle Fred with what I have got here." I pulled out the jewellery.

He had a look and said, "How much do you want?"

"I don't know, what do you think?" I asked.

"Well," he had a closer look and said, "I'll give you a hundred dollars and a bar tab for a couple of hours. Is that okay?"

I said, "Yeah, no problems." I probably had two thousand dollars' worth of jewellery there, but I knew not to disagree with him, he would do well on it.

So, he gave me the hundred dollars and said, "Head downstairs, I'll be down soon." The two girls in the room looked like they were going to finish whatever they were doing before I interrupted them.

Downstairs I went to the bar and got two drinks. I said, "I have a free tab. You can check if you like." She looked at me like I was joking. I said, "I'm Mick, Fred's nephew."

She suddenly changed her look and said, "Fine." And then gave me two drinks.

I was looking for Deb. She was watching a girl pole dancing. I said, "Hey."

She said, "I'd love to do that."

I laughed and said, "Well, I know the girls have a place out the back where they practice, do you want to have a go?"

"Fuck yeah!" She said.

I called over one of the girls I knew and told her. She said, "No, worries, come with me." We followed her out the back. A short time later, Deb learned some moves. She picked it up quickly, maybe too fast, lol, she was enjoying it.

I said, "Okay, we had better go; this girl had to get back to work." As we headed out, Fred came down the stairs and asked, "You going, Mick?"

"Yeah got things to do," I said.

"Okay, see you next time," he said as we started walking outside.

Heading back to the car, I had a bad feeling. Sure enough, we got to the corner and cops are there all over the car. I turned around and said, "Let's fuck off, right now." We walked to the train station.

I asked Deb, "Where to now?"

"Well, I have nowhere to go," she replied.

I said, "Same, well, why don't we just hop on a bus in the morning and head to Adelaide?" "Yeah, okay," she said.

We headed to Spencer street station and slept there waiting for the bus depot to open at 6 a.m. It was about midnight, so we had time to relax and talk. I could feel that the drugs were bringing me down.

I hated that feeling and the pain that was yet to come in my gut. I wasn't going to have that on the bus, so I had a bit more speed. That would keep me awake for the whole trip. Deb never used speed, only pot, which helped her sleep.

At 6 a.m., the depot opened. We went in and asked for any tickets to Adelaide. We bought them and boarded about an hour later. On the bus, I was looking out of the window with Deb's head on my shoulder, sleeping. I thought, *'What am I going to do when we get there?'* I had no plans, and I had no feelings for Deb. She's just a friend who I had sex with a couple of times; I could see she liked me. I would see what happens. Before too long, we were there.

It was my first time in Adelaide, so it was a bit exciting. We got off the bus, and Deb looked at me and said, "Where to now?"

I said, "I have no idea." I thought to myself, *'It's where she grew up so she should know.'*

"Well, I have an uncle who owns a tattoo shop where I got my boobs done, let's go see him, it's in the main street of town," she said.

"Okay," I said.

Walking down the main street, I noticed it was a lot smaller city than Melbourne, no tall buildings. It felt like a big country town.

We arrived at her Uncle Greg's tattoo shop. It was a very old building like it had been there for years and years. When you walked inside, it had all the old tattoos on the wall, not like how modern today's shops are. I thought there must have been a lot of people through this shop over the years. Deb yelled out to her uncle. He came out from behind a curtain that led to the back and said, "Well, well, Deb. How are you love?"

He looked like a big built bikie. He had ginger hair with white through it with a goatee, glasses and looked about sixty years old. I guess I maybe look older.

He looked at me and said to Deb, "And who may this be?"

She said, "Mick, I met him in Melbourne; we are travelling together."

"To what do I owe the pleasure?" He asked.

She looked at him with her big brown eyes and said, "Could you put us up for a day or two?"

I could see he wasn't that happy when she said that. "Well Deb darling if it were just yourself I would, but I can't you see, but you're welcome to hang around for the day."

She looked at me and said, "You want to do that?" I said,

"Yeah, okay." I needed time to think of what to do and where to go, as I only had about twenty dollars left on me.

We sat down, and Deb said to him, "Uncle, could you give Mick a tattoo?" I looked and thought, I only had two tattoos, and I would like one, but I couldn't pay for it.

She said, "Please!"

He said, "Okay, I'm not doing anyone at the moment, but if a customer comes in, we will have to stop and start again when I finish."

"Okay, fair enough," I said.

"What do you want, Mick?"

I said, "I have no idea. How about you do what you think okay."

He smiled. So, he started on my upper arm. No one had come in yet, so he was going for it.

He finished it and said, "Do you like it?"

Meeting Deb

"Yeah," I said.

It was a dragon and a knife, very old school, but it cost me nothing.

He said, "Well, no one has come in yet. I'll do another if you like?"

"Yeah, sure," I said.

"But first go to the shop and get a few cans of coke while Deb and I catch up."

I walked down to the shop, which was about a two-minute walk while looking at my new tattoo.

I entered the shop, and a customer walked in, and he started asking about a tattoo. He wanted a small one which would probably only take an hour to do. I told him to go to Deb's uncle.

Once I got back to the tattoo shop, I had a chance to talk to Deb and asked if she has any ideas on where to go tonight.

Deb said, "I have a girlfriend who lives in a suburb about an hour's ride on the bus. We can crash there."

"Okay, will she be home?" I said.

"Yeah she should be, I'll ring her on uncle's phone in a minute," Deb said.

"Cool," I said. This other guy had his tattoo done and walked out.

Her uncle said to me, "Well Mick, look through these books I have and if you see a tattoo you like I will do it for you. Take your time as I want to show some old pics in the family album to Deb of her mum to give her. We will be out the back, give us about thirty minutes or so."

I said, "Yeah okay," as I was keen to look through these tattoo books. I never thought there was anything strange going to happen.

He said, "If anyone comes in to give him a yell."

"Okay," I said.

Off they go behind this curtain and down the hall. About forty minutes go by, and no one has come into the shop. Deb came out and then the uncle.

"Did you find one?" He asks.

"Yes," I said.

He sets up his gear and hooks into it. After he finishes my tattoo, which was about two hours later, I said, "Did Deb tell you I can't pay you for these?"

"Yeah she told me, it's all good."

"Is there anything I could do like clean your shop or something?" I replied.

"Na, don't worry about it, but you guys better head off. I have got someone coming shortly," he said.

"Yeah okay, let's go, Deb," I said.

About a week later, Deb said to me, "You know the tattoos you had done?"

"Yes," I said.

"Well, you didn't have to pay for them because I paid."

"What, but you didn't have any money!" I said.

"I know, but I have other ways you can pay. When you were choosing your tattoo, Uncle Greg was making me suck his dick and wanting to play with me," she said.

Shocked, I said, "Are you kidding?"

"No," she said with tears in her eyes. "He used to do this to me when mum would go out to the pub and leave me with him."

Feeling dumb-founded, when I looked back on it now, I believed him about the looking at family photos. My mind

Meeting Deb

was too busy. I was excited about getting a tattoo. It never clicked to me on reading Deb's body language to see if she didn't look that happy as she went off with him, that dirty bastard.

Deb said, "Don't worry about it, there's nothing you can do. He has too many bikie mates, and they all think he's wonderful. They would get you if you did anything."

I felt sick when she told me this, but we left the shop that night and went to her girlfriend's place was home at the time. She was a pretty girl who had a one-year-old Asian featured little boy, so I gathered she must have an Asian boyfriend.

The first night there she said to us, "Well, I have only got my bed and baby's bed so you guys will have to sleep in my bed."

I thought she was going to sleep in the lounge.

I said, "We don't want to steal your bed."

She said, "No, you're right. I'll be okay sleeping next to you guys; it will be cool."

I thought *'Oh my god this could get interesting,'* and it did. We got into bed, and straight-up, Deb and her friend started going for it, kissing etc. I thought, *'Why not join in as well; that was my first threesome.'*

The next day I felt weird, but they seemed okay. Deb told me they used to have a thing, a few years ago and laughed at me, the way I had this strange look on my face. Again, that night, the same thing happened. I thought, *'God, I'm lucky.'* But on the third-night things were a lot different.

There was a knock on the door around 11 p.m. I could hear a few male voices.

This girl said, "Oh no, it's him."

I said, "Him, who?"

"It's my kid's father, quickly get dressed," she said.

I quickly got dressed and went to the toilet to pretend that's where I had been. Deb went into the lounge. Her friend went to the door and opened it.

She said, "Yeah, what do you want?"

He is Vietnamese and has three others with him. They were all drunk.

He said, "I'm here to see the boy."

She replied, "He is asleep."

"Out of the way," he said as he pushed his way through. He went into the lounge room and sat on the floor. I came out of the toilet.

He looked at me and said, "Who are you?"

"I'm with Deb, we're all good mate," I replied.

Well, he didn't look happy to see us there, and there was a bad feeling in the room. I sat down while they were on the floor, drinking tall bottles of beer and talking in their language. I didn't like it because I felt they were talking about me. It all made me feel uncomfortable. I could see Deb's friend was suddenly on edge as well.

After about only a minute, they began to get louder, and they weren't talking to us. I wasn't feeling good, so I thought maybe we should leave.

I said to Deb, "Come out the back so I can talk to you."

She got up, and we both went outside.

I said, "What do you think we should do?"

She said, "Well, let's go." Before she said anything else, we could hear her friend screaming out, "Go on get out!"

Meeting Deb

I said to Deb, "That doesn't sound good, let's get our gear and go."

She said, "Yeah, okay."

We headed back inside and here are these guys, they have got hold of her friend up against the wall hitting her.

I yelled: "Hey, leave her alone, you prick!"

They turned around, pushed me outside and said, "Shut up, you Aussie cunt!"

Well, I saw red and took a hit to one of them. I was outnumbered. The three guys started to hit me. I felt punches all over my body. I hit the ground and felt them kicking me. All I could hear was screaming, and it was scary, I thought, '*I'm fucked.*' It probably lasted a minute, but it felt more like ten.

They went inside, and I was left lying there, I couldn't move. Deb was crying and yelling at her friend, calling her all sorts of names. She grabbed our stuff which wasn't much, a backpack of clothes. I got up, and we left through the backyard gate and started walking.

Deb kept asking, "You okay?"

"I'll be right," I said.

I thought, '*What am I going to do now?*'

Then I remembered I had an uncle here in Adelaide. It was mum's brother Rob. I loved seeing him when I was younger. He was so funny, everything was a joke to him, and he never told you a story without it being funny.

Chapter 17

UNCLE ROB

Rob was the type of guy who should have been on stage. He was a real old Aussie type of guy. He had hardly any hair, blonde with a large nose, and he would even joke about it. His wife Cheryl was a nutter and a bit eccentric. She had this strange laugh, and she would get so excited about anything, but she was a lovely lady.

While growing up, mum would see them three or four times a year. She was close to Rob. I thought if I could find him, I probably could stay at his place for a few days to work out what to do with myself.

Deb kept saying, "Go to the hospital,"

I kept saying, "Nar, I'll be right. Let's find a phone box and look in the phone book for Uncle Rob."

We kept walking. On the next street, there was a phone box. We went in and started looking through the phone book. I found his name and phone number.

Uncle Rob was living at a place called Elizabeth. It was around twenty kilometres from where I used to live. When I rang the number, Aunt Cheryl answered.

I said, "Hi Aunt, it's Mick."

Meeting Deb

She was so excited, "Where are you?" She said. I could hear her getting louder, "Rob, it's Mick, come to the phone!" She screamed.

She was always lively. Rob was always telling her to calm down. Uncle Rob got on the phone and said, "Hi Mick, what are you doing here? Did you escape from Victoria?" That was his way of being funny.

"Yes, Uncle Rob, I was attacked and beaten; I'm at this place near the city. I have nowhere to go, could you come to pick me up please?" I said.

"Yeah, sure. Give me your location details. I'll come to get you?" He said.

"Uncle Rob, I have a girl with me too," I said.

"Yeah no worries," he said. You could tell he was pleased to hear from me.

Within an hour, he was there to pick us up. He was driving an old HQ Holden. It was white and in perfect condition. While we were driving to his place, he was telling me about his two boys who were around seven and ten years old. I was listening, still very sore and thinking about the fight.

Uncle Rob asked about what happened, and by that time, we were pulling into his place. His kids were running out to check me out.

Aunt Cheryl kissed me and said, "Oh my god, look at you, come with me."

Aunt Cheryl took me into the bathroom to repair me, as she put it, while Rob was chatting with Deb. Things seemed to be going well. That night Cheryl was trying to feed us. I wasn't hungry because of the drugs in my system. We slept in the lounge room on the floor on a blow-up bed.

The next morning the kids were up a making a noise, so I got up, and Rob said, "You want some breakfast?"

"Na Uncle, I'll have something a bit later," I said. But Deb hooked in.

Uncle Rob asks, "How long do you want to stay over here for?"

I said, with an undecided look, "I have no idea."

Rob said, "I can't have my nephew staying nowhere. How about I arrange a caravan to put in the yard, my mate owns one he will lend it to me. Just swing him a little cash and chuck in for food here, and you can stay here as long as you like. I'll help you, Mick."

I thought, *'Oh my god, I don't have any cash, no job, nothing. How am I going to do this?'* Rob got the caravan over the next day, thank god, as sleeping on the floor was so fucking hard.

At least we had a place to stay.

While in the van, I said to Deb, "We need cash and fast. I don't know my way around here. My other uncle back in Melbourne, Fred, remember him?"

She said, "Yeah, the strip club?"

I said, "Yeah him, well he has a mate in the city who owns a club maybe we go into the city tomorrow and ask him if you can work. Would you do pole dancing?"

She looked at me as if to say what the fuck yeah, I knew she wanted to do it, so the next day, in the late arvo we headed into the city.

I rang Fred and told him where I was and asked him who was in charge.

Meeting Deb

He said, "Ask for Bernie." So, off we went. It was at the top of town. When we got there, lights were blinking around the door entrance with a bouncer standing at the door too.

"G' day mate," I said.

He looked at me with eyes that could kill, a shaved-headed big cunt wearing a suit.

"Yeah, what do you want?" He said,

"Is Bernie in at all?" I asked.

"Yeah, why, who the fuck are you?" He asked, looking at me as if to say, *this better be good,* or I will kick your ass.

I said, "Well, he is a friend of my uncle and he told me to call in and see him.

He went away and came back. "Go inside, walk through to the back and knock on the green door, not the red door," he said.

"Okay yeah mate," I said.

In the back of this place, as Deb and I entered, we saw girls dancing, barmaids and a few guys in there. I knocked on the green door, and a voice yelled: "Come in."

We walked in, and he said, "Hello sweetheart, and who the fuck are you?" I was a little scared. This guy looked like some crime boss.

I said, "You, Bernie?"

"Yeah, well if I'm not, I'm in big shit sitting in this chair."

"Well I am Mick, and this is Deb, you're friends with my Uncle Fred in Melbourne."

He started laughing and said out loud, "How's the old cunt, fuck it's been a while since I have seen him. It was in jail at Yalta. I helped him set up over in Melbourne to keep him out of jail. Your uncle is a mad prick and his nephew, well, well."

He picked up the phone and rang Fred at his club.

He said, "Hey, you old prick. I have your nephew Mick here, you know about this?"

They talked for a minute or so, then he hung up and said, "You're good. So, what is it you want?"

"Well Deb here has only a little experience in pole dancing, and we need money badly, we only just arrived. We are staying out of town."

"Yeah, yeah, don't go on, Well girly, take your top off and your bra and give me a look at what you have," he said.

She looked at me. I said, "Just do it." So she took it all off. Straight away he saw her fully tattooed boobs.

Looking, he said, "Who did them?"

"My uncle at the bottom of the street," she said in a quiet voice.

"What the grey-haired old perv who should have been shot years ago?" He asked.

"Yeah, that sounds right," Deb said.

Bernie looks at both of us.

"Are you both together?" He asked.

I straight-up thought he probably wouldn't like it if I said yes, as we weren't anyway. "No way, Bernie, we are mates just travelling together."

"Oh? Just fuck buddies," he laughs. "Well, you can start tonight. I will put you with one of the girls. The customers should love looking at your tits.

You, Mick, can go have a drink on the house, but you can't stay around when she's working, as I have had blokes

Meeting Deb

here before go all funny with their girlfriends showing their bits okay."

"Yeah, okay, Bernie," I said.

So I headed to the bar to get a drink while I was waiting for Deb, as she was off to learn the ropes. After an hour went by, she came back out.

"Okay, we can go," she said all excited as we hopped on the bus.

Heading back, we talked about her job.

On arriving home to Rob's, he said, "Have you been looking for work, Mick?"

"Yeah," I said.

"Well, I have got the barbecue on. Are you hungry?"

I was hungry this time because it had been two days since I had eaten, and I was feeling good.

That night a car pulled up out the front of the house.

I said to Deb, "Who's this?"

She said, "I gave Bernie this address to pick me up from to start work."

I was panicking, "What, why? Do that and my uncle Rob will flip out! What am I going to say?" I said.

Just as I said that Rob said, "Who's this guy?"

I thought, '*It's Bernie; he is some bouncer, I guess.*'

He is a friend of Deb's. He has come to take her to a friend of his. It is a place where they want a bar girl at a tavern." I said.

He looked out of the window and turned to me, saying, "Mick, I don't want trouble."

"No trouble," I said.

Deb went to work, and I sat home in the caravan, freaking out as I had no drugs, and it was doing my head in, which is what it does to you. The next morning around 5 a.m. Deb came in and put money on the table. She said, "You will be okay now."

Pacing the yard, trying to kill time until I could head to the mall to score, my anxiety was overwhelming. By the time I arrived home, Deb was asleep. Uncle Rob was at work, and his kids were at school. I was on a rush, so I started cleaning Rob's kitchen. I was mopping and cleaning the bathroom when suddenly Aunt Cheryl woke up.

"What are you doing, Mick?" She asked.

I said, "I thought I would clean the house for you."

She said, "Oh my god Mick, you're so sweet."

If only she knew that I was on speed and when you're on a high, you can go and go all day. When I was coming back down would be terrible, so I would make sure I would have a bit of pot to help with that.

Anyway, Cheryl said, "Where is Deb, and what time did she get home?"

I told her she was asleep and she got home at about 5 a.m.

"She works late, the pubs are not open here that late," she said.

Oops, I thought I fucked up; oh well, I changed the subject and started to vacuum the lounge room.

Cheryl was still in her long T-shirt, watching me having a coffee. She would sometimes flirt with me. I would think, *'Is she or do I think she is?'* But I was right. As I took a break, she suddenly jumped on me and wanted to rough me up.

She sometimes acted like a kid. Rob was always telling her to stop acting up and grow up. Cheryl would razz him

Uncle Rob

up. But this time she was doing it to me. So I was wrestling with her on the floor, and suddenly she kissed me. I went along with that, but things went too far next thing I know I'm fucking my Aunt. It was strange, but she's married to my Uncle Rob, my mum's brother.

After that, I was feeling horrible. Cheryl got up and said, "Don't tell your uncle about this."

I thought, '*As if I would.*' I went out to the van and stayed there all day, smoking pot to come down off the speed. I tried to sleep, but I just couldn't. I played music on my headphones and went into my world, which I loved.

Later that arvo Deb woke up and asked: "What have you been doing?" I said, "Cleaning." "Okay, I will get up and have a shower now," she said. But this meant going inside. I said, "Okay." So, I went inside to keep an eye on everything. I was feeling paranoid, but Cheryl was playing music loud and drinking. She appeared quite happy.

"Hi Micky," she said as if everything was fine.

Deb headed to the bathroom, had her shower, came out and headed back to the van.

Uncle Rob pulled up and said, "G'day, what have you been up to?"

"Nothing," I said, feeling guilty. I felt strange, and I didn't like this feeling. I headed to the van, and after dinner, Deb got ready to go to work, off she went.

I didn't want to sit around here, I got dressed, had a few lines on the table and left to head into the city. I went to see how Deb was going. I caught a bus which took about an hour to get there and went in.

Entering the club, I saw Deb doing her thing, stripping. I felt strange. Here she was doing this and giving me money.

I felt like I was a pimp, is that what I am doing now? I felt like I'm a bit of a prick.

I didn't stay long. I went to another bar to play pool and to take my mind off a few things like Cheryl and Deb. Playing a game of pool with these two guys. I was doing well. I always was a good pool player. These two guys didn't like losing and asked if I was from around here. I said, "No, from Melbourne."

They didn't like interstate rivalry because of football. Both states hated each other because of it, which gave them the fuel to hate me more. They started on me about that and said I should leave. I said, "I'll leave when I want to." Then a punch, I took that and said, "Fuck off!"

One guy went to hit me again, but I blocked that punch and grabbed his arm. I swung his head down onto the pool table, grabbed my cue and swung it right into the other guy's head, knocking him to the ground. They calmly walked out. Before security came, I left and got on a bus and went home to Robs.

As I get into my caravan van, Rob knocked on my door.

"Mick, you there?"

"Yes," I said, shitting myself.

"I want to talk to you," he said.

I wondered what Cheryl had said.

"Yes Rob, what is it?" I asked.

"Does this belong to you?" He said, as he showed me a bag of weed and two bags of speed. He pointed at the table, and there was a line there. I thought, *'Oh no I can't believe I was so dumb to leave that lying around, I didn't think they would come out to the van.'*

Uncle Rob

Rob said, "Your aunt came out here to change your sheets and to collect your washing, she saw this on the table, and she was freaking out over it.

I quickly said, "It's not mine; it's Deb's. I warned her about this."

Rob said, "Come inside."

"Okay," I said and followed him inside.

Aunt Cheryl was crying, sitting at the kitchen table.

Rob said to her, "Don't worry love, it's not Mick's it is hers."

I was standing there looking at Cheryl, her eyes looked terrible, she looked up at me and said, "That's good, you can stay, but she will have to go."

"Okay," I said.

When Deb got home around 6 a.m. as soon as she walked in, I said, "I'm going out, and when I get back, you are not to be here."

"Why?" She said.

"Because I told them the drugs, they found were yours," I told her.

"Thanks," she said.

I went out and caught a bus to the beach, which was about an hour and a half away. I swam, had lunch and caught the bus back. When I walked into the yard, I went to the van. Deb wasn't there, her things were gone, and I never saw her again.

I thought, *'That's good, but she's gone now, I have no money. What am I going to do? Fuck, I will have to look for a job, fuck that.'*

Chapter 18

Gay Encounter

For the next three weeks, I stayed with my aunt and uncle. Rob was good as far as feeding me but was on my back to find a job. "Everything would be better," he kept saying, but I didn't want a job. I didn't know what I was going to do; a job to me was something different. I was always making money the easy way; that was my thing.

In those last three weeks, Cheryl tried to get her way with me again, but I couldn't do it. I wasn't wasted on any drugs anymore, so it was easy to push her away. I had always done stupid things when under the influence of drugs. While on drugs, it's as though you don't care and you don't think about what is right and what is wrong.

I left South Australia and caught a bus back to Melbourne. I didn't even say goodbye to Uncle Rob. He was at work, but still, I was a cunt to him and didn't want to see him and feel the guilt, so it was easier to fuck off. I hate it when you know you have done something wrong and the way you think about it in your head. It messes with your head.

Arriving in Melbourne, I had no idea what I was going to do or where I was going to go?

It would be so easy to see the crew and start work, again. It would be easy to see Fred for some work, but I didn't want to be in that scene anymore. Maybe it was time to go straight. I hadn't thought about it that way before.

I caught a train to my mate Warren's place. He was a guy with a van. Maybe I could crash there a few nights? I headed there, and he was happy to see me and asked if I was on my own.

"Yes," I said.

"Okay," you can crash here, but please, only a week, you need to get your life together! He said.

"I know," I said. I then had a shower to freshen up.

We sat and talked for a while. Warren asked me what had been going on. I filled him in and also told him about my Aunt.

He went, "Oh my god, you didn't?"

"Yeah, shame, hey?" I said.

The next morning, I was up ready to go looking for a job. '*A job, who me?*' I thought. So off I went to a few places, no luck. I called around to see a couple of my footy mates, to catch up. They were having a barbecue and a few drinks. They were smoking pot too. Cool, I fitted straight in. I must have been away for a few days.

Later on, I went back to Warren's. When I got there, he said he had something to tell me. Straight away, I thought he wants me to leave. "Okay, what is it?" I asked. What he came out with was a big surprise. "Well, while you were away, I had a couple come over for a few days, they are from work, and I had sex with them."

I said, "That's nothing, you had a threesome, then, I said."

He said, "Yes but I had sex with both of them, a girl and her boyfriend, so I'm gay. I should tell you because when you come out of the shower with just a towel around you, it is turning me on."

I was making a coffee at the time while he was telling me. I suddenly stopped and thought, *'What the fuck?'* I quickly said, "Stop, I need to go out for a walk. I'll be back later."

He said, "Okay, I understand it's a shock for you. I will see you later."

I was out of there real quick. I headed back to the boys place where they were still drinking. I walked in, and one of them said, "Are you okay, Mick? You look like you have seen a ghost." I said loudly, "He is gay!"

Everything went quiet. "Who's gay?" They asked. I said, "Warren." "Hey, what? Start again. What has happened?" They asked confusedly.

I told them what he had said to me, and all four of them said: "Yeah, well, we were always suspicious of him."

I asked, "What do you mean?"

"Well just the way he is, his lifestyle, he keeps to himself," they said. I still didn't know what they meant. Anyway, I sat down in the lounge and started drinking again, laughing about it all.

The only thing was the boys started stirring me up about it saying things like, "Did he try and sneak into your bed and suck your dick? "Was he a good kisser?" Stuff like that. But the trouble was, the more they stirred me up, the more I was starting to get angry about him dumping that on me while I was staying there.

After the boys gave me more shit about it, I got up and walked out saying, "See ya!"

They yelled, "Where are you going?"

Gay Encounter

I kept walking and headed to Warren's. After about a ten-minute walk, I arrived there, and he was sitting on the lounge.

I walked in and said, "I have come to get my bag of clothes, and I'm out of here."

He looked at me and said, "You don't have to leave."

We started to fight over it.

I said, "I don't care what sex you like, but to put it on me, that's something else."

He went to grab me, and I took a swing at him. Well, I also found out that poofs can fight, the furniture went flying along with the punches. I went straight through the window, head first. That was when the fighting stopped.

I got up, and I was yelling.

He said, "You're bleeding pretty badly." I ripped off my T-shirt and wrapped it around my head. I started to head back to see the boys. As I walked in, they got a shock as the blood had soaked through the T-shirt. I still thought I would be okay, but I wasn't.

The boys said, "Jump into the shower and wash the blood off." When I did wet my forehead, I found had a cut right across my head. It was about four inches long and as wide as my thumb, I knew this was bad.

The boys were too drunk to drive me to the hospital, so they called an ambulance. When I arrived at the hospital, I needed about thirty stitches and had to stay in overnight. The next day I could hardly see, one eye swollen closed and the other half shut, I was black and blue, a real mess. I caught a taxi back to the boys' place as I had nowhere else to go. They would have all crashed out from the big night, so I thought I would see what happened.

As the taxi pulled up, I got out, only to see two cop cars pulled up in front of me. Walking into my mates' yard, they yelled "Stop" and walked over to ask what had happened to me.

I said, "It's okay; just got into a fight at the park last night."

"Bullshit, you follow us!" The cop said.

We started walking along the footpath, following this blood trail. I wondered where this is going to lead. As we got a couple of houses away from Warren's, one of the cops said, "Well, you want to tell us the truth because we know what has happened?" So, I started telling them how he was a mate, and how he put it on me and that he was gay and we started to fight.

"Okay, let's go to the station. We are going to charge you as Warren told us a different story." One of them said. So, we headed down to the station where I am making a statement about what happened. I was sitting there, and after three or four hours, the cop came in and said, "You're free to go, he dropped the charges against you." I thought, *'What do you mean?'*

"Warren rang us and said he doesn't want to charge you, he was just angry with you. You guys can sort it out, so get out of here." I thought, *'Fuck yeah and walked outside the station.'*

As I got outside, I hear this voice yell out, "Mick." I looked over and saw it was my mate, Rob. I was wondering what he was doing here and how he knew I was there. I jumped into his car; it was an old beat-up XC Ford. I asked him how he knew I was here. He told me the boys at the house saw the cops take me away and rang him because they were still too drunk to drive.

He said he went around to Warren's to see him and told him to drop the charges on me. Warren said "no." He then grabbed him and wrapped the phone cord around his neck and said, "You ring and drop the charges before I choke the fuck out of you." As I was choking him, he decided to listen and rang. I told him what to say, and that's why you are out.

Warren said, "As long as he never sees you again, he will be fine with it all, no problems." I was amazed Rob did this and thanked him. "No worries mate," he said. He asked me to come to stay with him and his girlfriend for a while, so I did.

Chapter 19

CLOSE TO DEATH

We arrived at Rob's place, he lived in one of those old narrow houses joined together, called terrace houses. It was probably eighty or ninety years old, a lot of people buy them and renovate them, which is what Rob was doing. Rob's girlfriend was weird. She was more educated and worked in the city. She thought she was smarter and better than you, where Rob was a working-class, drug dealer.

I could never understand how they were a match because they were both opposite types of people. She made me feel uncomfortable the way she spoke, so I didn't want to stay long, but Rob loved having me there. I helped him with his renovating. We put up a front fence and did some painting. At night we would have a few bourbons, get stoned and make a feed. He didn't eat meat, so he used to go to a vegetarian place in the city to get his food, it was a Hari Krishna restaurant.

Once I went there with him. As I entered, I saw a book on a shelf with a picture of John Lennon and George Harrison, from The Beatles. I picked it up and started to read while eating and found it very interesting. Appreciating the peace these people had and what the book was saying, I thought nothing more. About six months later, this experience came back and hit me big time.

Staying back at Rob's place, I thought, '*What am I going to do with myself?*' One day I headed into Footscray which was about eight stations away, on the train. I wondered who I was. I was feeling lost. I got off the train and headed to the mall. I thought I know so many people here something good will come out of this day.

Sure enough, it did, but not what I thought it would turn out to be. I looked over and who do I see? Danny from the days working for the Chinese. He seemed terrible, not like last time I saw him wearing the best of clothes and jewellery. Now he was wearing old clothes, no jewellery and his face looked thin. He looked like a zombie.

I walked over and said, "Danny, how's things? Long-time mate."

He was happy to see me. "Mick, what the hell are you doing?" He said.

We went to a pub and had a beer. We were talking shit. I asked about him the Chinese thing. "What did you tell the cops? I got dragged in over it." I said. He wasn't interested in talking about it. I noticed he changed the subject, so we drank some more. The pub in Footscray is one where the nasty type of people get rough, and things can get very colourful quickly. It was called the Royal Hotel for those who know Footscray.

We came out of there around 5 p.m., and I felt like I was a bit tipsy and feeling cheeky kind of mood. I asked Danny, "What you feel like doing now?"

He said, "Why don't we grab a few from the bottle shop and go around to our old mate Steve's?"

I said, "Good idea. He will have some pot as well, should be a good night."

Danny said, "I have just got to go to the mall first to see this Asian guy about getting on?" He was talking about heroin.

I was a bit pissed off that he needed to do that, as I never used that shit, but I said, "Yeah okay, Danny."

We headed off. We got about five hundred yards down the road where all the Chinese restaurants and pizza shops are. It was a good place to get a feed as there were lots of them. It was on Barkly Street. Suddenly a new car pulled alongside us, and two guys in suits jumped out and yelled, "Hey, you two." They were cops, and they flashed their badges.

We turned and said, "What the fuck have we done?"

One said, "Are you Danny?" Looking straight at him.

Danny said, "Yeah, what?"

"Come with us the two of you." They said.

We looked at each other, thinking, *'What the fuck?'*

Before we could say anything, they had handcuffed us both and put us in the back of this car.

We were asking them, "Where are we going?"

"You will see," they replied.

We noticed they weren't heading towards the Footscray cop shop and not towards the city. So again we asked where we were going and asking what had we done.

They just said, "You will find out."

I was shitting myself. We started to get further away from the suburbs. We were out near Werribee, which is about thirty kilometres out of Footscray, after Werribee. It was just bush; it wasn't looking good. Danny was quiet as if he knew something.

I looked at him and asked, "What do you know?"

He turned to me and said, "I think this is bad."

'Great, what has he got me into?' I thought.

Suddenly they go down this dirt road for about three kilometres. There was a river and a barbecue area there. I am thinking about what is going to happen.

I yelled at these two, "You're not cops, are you?"

"Shut up if you know what's good for you," they shouted back.

We came to a stop. The men pulled me out of the car first.

I was yelling "Can you just tell me what I have done?" No answer, just a hit in the head and pushed behind the car.

They walked me over to a tree where they handcuffed me to the tree. Leaving me to fetch Danny; they both started to kick and punch the shit out of him. I could see Danny covered in blood and screaming out, but couldn't make out what he was saying.

I heard one of these blokes say, "You think you're smart fucking with Kong. Well, Kong said hello." I knew that it was the Chinese Kong, the guy with the scruffy suit, the shady one, the one who I didn't like. I thought they must have caught up with Danny.

They must have been watching him for a while. Stupid me, happened to be in the wrong place at the wrong time. Danny is yelling, "Don't kill me you fucking assholes! Please stop!"

But they kept hitting him. I noticed they were using a baton made of leather, it was black and red, about a foot long, something like the cops used to use in the old days. I am shitting myself. *'Are they going to kill us both?* I thought.

They gave him a rest and walked over to me and said: "You hang with scum; this is what you get." They started to hit me with this baton. It felt like an iron bar was hitting me. They hit my ribs with this baton. I heard them crack. I felt the baton hit behind my legs. I felt as though I had been run over.

While one guy was doing that the other punched me in the face. I was down on the ground for only ten or fifteen minutes but seemed like an hour or two. They took the handcuffs off me, but I couldn't move. I laid still pretending to be passed out, and I felt another hit. I looked over to see them give Danny a couple more kicks in the head then they left him there and drove off. I was so glad to see them drive off. For now, I knew I was going to live.

Slowly, I crawled over to Danny. I was about fifty feet away and said, "Danny, say something." He wasn't moving, his eyes were closed, and there was no response. I started to yell "Danny wake up." On shaking him he made a groan, I held him. I couldn't get up as my legs were in so much pain.

All I could do was sit, wait and hope someone would drive into this area. It just kept getting darker. Who was going to be out here this time of day? I sat and waited, getting colder. I was wondering what Danny had said to the cops in Queensland. It must have been enough for the Chinese to hire these guys to bust him up.

Whether they were meant to kill him or bust him up, I wasn't sure. Danny wasn't moving, and I couldn't feel any life in his body. I put my ear to his chest and couldn't hear a heartbeat; I thought he was dead. I started to cry and cry like a little boy. I thought to myself, *'How was I going to get out of here? Am I going to die too?'* I was so cold.

I crawled to the river and washed my face and my body to get some of the blood off me. I crawled back to Danny to recheck him, still nothing. I lay next to him through the night to keep warm. I could hear noises in the bush. Animals, I thought, but what kind? Would they smell blood and get me? Wondering what the worst animal out here might be. Foxes perhaps, as we didn't have wolves or bears. Lucky because I was panicking all night.

I fell asleep for an hour, maybe. I had no idea what time it was. I was looking around for any form of human life. But I hadn't seen one car, any headlights, nothing, it was so quiet. I was feeling so sore. I reckon I had a couple of ribs broken. My legs were burning with pain. *'Hurry up, morning,'* I thought.

It seemed forever, the sunrise was coming, and birds were everywhere. I started to feel Danny, but he was as cold as ice. I knew he was dead. I thought I couldn't do anything for him. I am going to have to leave him here. I didn't want to, but I had to start saving myself.

Seeing a few fallen tree branches laying on the ground, I thought I could use one to help me walk. I had to get out of here. I grabbed a thick branch and snapped the end off, as it was too long. Taking off my shirt, I wrapped it on one end to place under my arm like a crutch. That worked, so I started to limp away, looking back around seeing Danny laying there.

After five minutes of walking, I couldn't see him anymore. I was still crying. Seeing him, knowing he was dead. But I just needed to focus and use all my strength to get out of there.

What would I say if a car comes? Do I tell them the truth? I didn't want to end up at a cop shop telling them what happened? What if they were cops and they worked on the Chinese books? What if I saw them there? They might not have wanted to kill us, or maybe they thought they did. My mind was racing. I didn't know what the right thing to do was, so I kept walking, it was so painful.

Suddenly a four-while drive Ute was coming; an old farmer was driving. He pulled up and said to me, "Are you, alright mate?"

I said, "No, mate, I'm not."

"You want a lift anywhere?" He asked.

"Yeah," I said and hopped in.

"Shit mate, you need a hospital. What has happened to you?" He asked.

I had to think of a lie to tell him. I didn't need him to be suspicious.

I said, "My mates and I were at a farmhouse having a party and things turned nasty, too much to drink and fights broke out. I received the worst of it, so I just started to walk home."

"Well, mate, you must have some terrible mates to do that to you," he said.

"Yeah," I said with relief. I was just in a car getting away but wondered who and when someone would find Danny.

The farmer drove me into town and said, "Mate, I should drop you off at the hospital."

I said, "Yeah, OK."

So he dropped me off out the front of the hospital, and I said, "Thanks mate for the lift."

After he drove away, I headed towards the train station, as much as I needed to go to the hospital, I knew there would be too many questions asked, and the cops would get involved. That was the last thing I wanted.

Feeling scared, I thought I would go to someone's place to rest and decide what I would do later. I needed a hot shower and to get my injuries sorted. Sitting at the train station for a while, eventually, the train pulled in. I hopped on board. The train was heading towards the city. I might go to my Uncle Fred's place; he lived in Yarraville, an old part of Melbourne. If he were home, I could stay there. I know if I told him what had happened, he would know what I should do.

Arriving at his place, I knocked on the door, and he was home. He opened the door and said, "What the fuck has happened to you? Come in." I just made it and fell into a seat, glad to be off my feet and to relax. I told him in detail what had happened. He was amazed I was alive.

He said, "These guys probably thought you were dead or thought you would be not far from it, who knows, but I can tell you one thing, you need to forget about it. You will regret going to the cops. The attention you would bring could be dangerous for you."

I thought he was probably right.

It felt so good to be clean and warm after I had a shower. I couldn't stand, I just sat in the shower for about ten minutes.

After I got out, Fred asked, "Do you want a feed or drink?"

I said, "No, I can't, I feel sick, but I'd love a coffee and a smoke."

He made me a coffee, and we sat out the back. He looked at me and said, "Stay here as long as you need and when you feel better come into work and get a job." "Thanks, Fred," I said.

My uncle started to get himself ready to head into the club. He said he had shit to do and told me to rest up and he would see me later that night.

"If you need me just use the phone and ring the club," he said.

"Yep, I will, Uncle." Then off he went.

As I sat in his place, all I wanted to do was sleep. I fell asleep for a while but not for long as the pain kept me awake. My ribs were killing me every time I breathed in or out, it was agony, like being hit all over again. My head and legs were still hurting. I got up looking for some pain killers but couldn't find any, so I rang Fred.

He asked if I was coping alright, and I said I needed some pain relief.

He said, "Well, I am a bit busy at the moment, but I will send one of my girls over, she will get whatever you need, okay?"

About an hour later, a car pulled up, and there was a knock at the door. It was one of the girls from the club, I knew her, and she had been working there for quite a while. Her name was Gaylene. She was tall, blonde, about eighteen years old, a very nice woman.

She took one look at me and said, "Oh my god Mick, who did this to you? Your eyes are so bruised."

I said, "Well, I don't want to talk about it. Did you bring anything?"

"Yeah, I have Valium in my bag, which will knock you out," she said.

"Yeah okay, but I need something for the pain," I said.

"Okay," she said, looking at me, worried.

I could see she was acting like a mother when her child gets hurt.

"Let me look at you; I can help. Fred said I could stay with you as long as you need me."

I said, "Thanks, could you go to the chemist and get me the strongest tablets you can find and grab me a burger and a coke?"

She rushed to the chemist with a worried look on her face.

About an hour later, she was back with my food and medicine.

"Here you go, anything else? "She said.

I am feeling so hungry. I was looking into the burger, shaking my head.

"No, all good," I said.

She said, "I will run a bath for you."

I said, "No, I will be right." But she ran the bath anyway. I finished my feed, had my tablets and thought, '*Why not? I will have that bath.*'

So, I stripped off in front of Gaylene and got into the bath. I just laid there thinking this feels much better, while Gaylene grabbed the soap and helped wash me.

When I was ready to get out the bath, she said, "I will give you a gentle massage." I laid on my uncle's bed. She had the softest hands massaging my legs, it hurt but was a good hurt. She did this for an hour. Feeling much more relaxed, I must have fallen asleep. I woke up, and it was dark. I yelled out to Gaylene, but there was no answer, she must have gone.

I noticed a note next to me; it read, *"Hi Mick, I left you to sleep. If you need anything at all, ring me. Here is my number anytime, okay. Love, Gaylene."*

I thought, '*How sweet,*' but I never did ring her. Instead, I rang my uncle, he answered.

"Yeah, it's me, Mick," I said.

"How are you feeling now," he asked? "Yeah still fucked but better after Gaylene came and helped me," I told him.

"Yeah she's a good scout," he replied. "Well, I will be home at about 3 a.m. I will see you then," he said.

"Okay, Fred," I said. I hung up the phone and fell back to sleep. I got up around 1 a.m. I would wait up for Fred. It was about 2 a.m. when he walked in.

"You're awake," he said.

"Yeah, just having a coffee and a smoke," I replied.

Fred smelt of grog and perfume. As he walked past me, he said, "I will see you when I wake up."

"Okay, Fred," I said.

He turned and said, "I forgot, I have this for you." It was a bag of pot, "This might help you as I know you love smoking this shit," he said, and off he went. I rolled a joint and chilled; that's what I needed. I went out back, and within five minutes, I was in my place. A place that made me feel good and I didn't give a fuck about anything that had happened. I finished my joint and went and laid down again. I was sleeping a lot, my body probably telling me to do that so I could heal, I guess.

The next day I was still sore but a little better. I was walking a bit better as well. I would get out and go for a walk to the corner shop if you could call it walking. It was more like limping. I felt like an iced coffee and maybe buy a newspaper. So off I went, I got back to Fred's house, sat down, opened my iced coffee and started to read the newspaper. The page headlines said: *Body found in bushlands outside Werribee,* police *believe it's a murder.* Oh fuck I nearly choked on my iced coffee.

Getting up, I knocked on the door of Fred's room, "Uncle Fred," I shouted out. No answer, so I knocked again.

He yelled out, "Not yet. I'm still sleeping,"

I am freaking out.

"But Fred, I need to tell you something important," I said.

"Yeah, yeah, give me a minute," he said.

He came out, rubbing his eyes.

"Yeah, Mick, what the fuck! I need more sleep, make it quick, what is it?"

I showed him the newspaper. Well, he rubbed his eyes again and soon woke up when he saw the headlines.

"Oh, shit Mick, they're saying murder," he said.

"I know what should I do?" I asked him.

He said, "You need to move on. Can you go to your mums? Is she still in Queensland?"

I said, "Yes, yeah, okay."

Fred said, "But do it quickly, okay."

So, I thought another joint would calm me down, and then I'll ring mum. I gave it an hour and rang mum. She was surprised to hear from me.

"Mick, how are you? "She said.

"Yeah alright, mum, I'm thinking of coming up to see you," I said.

"Really? Well, Peter and I are moving down your way next week on the border of Victoria and South Australia," she told me.

"Oh really mum, okay, well I will catch up with you after you move then," I said before saying goodbye. I thought, '*I shouldn't go up there as I have a warrant out on me. That would be like walking into the lion's den. What am I going to do?*'

After a few hours, Fred gets up and asks, "Did you ring your mum?"

"Yeah, I can't go up there. I have a warrant; I remembered," I said.

"Oh true, well, don't go there," he answered.

"Well, can I still stay here for a while?" I asked.

"Yeah, but only until you can get around better," he said.

I just had to get better and think about where I am going. After about two weeks, I was getting around. Fred asked if I wanted a job. I asked him what I would be doing. He told me to come into the club to talk about it. Later that night, I entered the club with him and recognised a few faces. We headed up to his office.

"Grab a seat, Mick," he said. Could you take my car and run the girls home, the ones that finish and pick a couple of girls up?" He asked. "Yeah, no problems," I said. I did that and got back and asked, "Is there anything else you want me to do?"

He looked up. I could tell he was thinking. "Well, Mick, I have been thinking about what you could do around here. There isn't much as the customers don't like guys behind the bar and you're not fit enough to be one of my bouncers. So I'm going to have to say, it's time to move on." I knew he was thinking about himself with all the dramas I had, and he didn't need the attention.

He said, "You will be alright," and handed me an envelope.

"What's this?" I asked.

He said, "It's a little something to help you."

"Thanks, Fred, you have helped me enough already." I said.

He was kind, and it was his way of saying disappear. I walked out of his place not knowing at the time that it would be the last time I saw him because our paths never crossed again and I just never stayed in touch.

As I walked down the street, I looked in the envelope. It had a $1000 in it. I didn't know how to feel. I and just kept walking thinking, '*Now what? Where do I go?*' I decided to go straight back to my crew in Williamstown.

I headed to the club and walked in. I got some looks, some good and some I wasn't sure. I went to the bar and had a drink when all of a sudden I hear: "Well, well, if it isn't Mick. Where have you been?" It was Ray, the boss. I said with a rusty voice, "Working in the city for my uncle."

He knew my uncle but not his phone number, they weren't that close. If he saw him, he would say, "Hi."

He said, "Well, where are you staying at the moment?"

I said, "Nowhere just now, I thought I would ask you if there is anything I could do for you. I need cash and a place to stay."

He looked at me. I felt strange, as though I had done something wrong, but I hadn't. Probably the only thing was not staying in touch. They get shitty over that, and you don't know what they have been doing. They won't tell you anything until you're around a lot. I understand, but it makes it hard because you are left feeling paranoid.

The boss said, "Well, hang around, have a yarn, and I will think what you can do, alright?"

I said, "Okay."

He said to me, "Did you hear about Danny? They discovered his body at Werribee, murdered not long ago."

"Yeah," I said, feeling paranoid.

Then he said, "What about Hughsie? He was murdered, as well. We are all getting popped off."

"Yeah," I said.

I thought to myself he was only talking the gossip, and I then stopped feeling paranoid. Hughsie was a druggie who killed another person. We all knew Deaba, and he was a druggie too. Deaba went to score for Hughsie and had a taste out of his bag.

When he met up to give him his bag, Hughsie could tell it was light and started to fight with Deaba. He punched him to the ground, and he died. The cops found out who did it and charged him. He did some time I jail, got out and was only out for like two months when suddenly he is dead, found in a schoolyard.

Someone gave him a hot shot which was heroin with shit in it to kill him, and that was the score there. I knew both of them well since school days. Ray walked away drinking with the boys. I was feeling a bit weird. '*Maybe it was a bad idea coming here,*' I thought to myself.

Ray said, "Come outback. I want to talk to you?"

I wondered what it was going to be about, you never know with him. I have known people to go away with him and never to be heard of again.

There was a pier out the back door of this club and a boat where they would go fishing. I knew I hadn't done anything wrong, so I felt safe. We walked outside. Ray said he had a job I might be interested in, and I was all ears.

"I have got a house over on Phillip Island. It's empty; I have only been using it as a place to go on holidays fishing, and it needs some stuff doing to it like painting etc. I can't get any of the other boys to go there as they have families now and there's no work.

So I thought you could go there and stay rent-free and do the renovations I want doing. I will come down whenever I can and drop off materials to do whatever needs doing. This way, we both get what we want," he explained to me.

I thought, *'This sounds good.'* I said, "Yeah, sure, sounds perfect."

He continued to say, "There's one other thing, there is a guy I will give you his number. He is a fisherman friend of mine. He knows everyone down there.

When you head down there, I will give you a pound of hash to take to him. In a week you come back here and give me the cash for it. What you and he make out of it is your business." I thought, *'Okay this is sounding better.'*

"When do you want me to head off?" I asked him.

"Well, stay here tonight, and in the morning you can head there. How are you going to get there? He said.

I said, "I don't know as I don't have wheels."

"Yeah, well I will get one of the boys to drive you, but you're going to need a car as soon as possible," he said.

Chapter 20

LIVING ON AN ISLAND

The next morning, I was off in a car with a guy who worked for Fred. It took about three hours to get there. It was a seldom-used old holiday house which needed a good coat of paint. The fence palings were broken and rotten, and the house generally, needed a good overhaul, inside and out. I checked it out as soon as we got there.

The other guy said, "Well, I have got a long drive back; I will leave you with it."

"Yeah, okay," I said.

I could see it had everything I needed, a bed, a fridge, plates, knives, forks, blankets, sheets and a washing machine. I was thinking, *'This is turning out to be a good thing after all. I can lay low here.'* So, I quickly settled in.

The next day there was a knock on the door it was this fisherman.

"G' day mate, I'm Fizz," he said, "You must be Mick?"

"Yeah, mate," I answered.

"Well, have you got the hash?" He asked me.

"Yeah, mate," I said.

Did Ray tell you how much he wants at his end?" He asked.

"Yeah, "Two and a half grand," I replied.

"Cool, will you help me break it down and then we will head to the pub where you just sit there and do whatever and I will get onto selling some," he told me.

I said, "Yeah, sure mate no problems."

So, we cut it up into quarters and even singles.

I said, "That's a lot of singles, will you be able to sell all of it in a week?"

"Yeah, easy," he said.

So, we head down to the pub with about an ounce. The pub was a nice place with fishing pictures on the walls of sharks and boats etc. It was a working-class pub with a betting area. I was happy about this as I had always loved a bet. I headed in there and left Fizz to do what he needed to do. After an hour, he came in looking for me.

"Are you ready?" He asked.

I said, "Yeah, I'm not winning much."

"Well, let's head back to the house. I need more," he said.

I said, "What? It's only been an hour, and you have sold an ounce of singles, fuck me that was quick."

I grabbed a six-pack of beers and headed back to the house. Fizz loved Bourbon, so he grabbed a bottle of Bourbon and off we went.

We started walking back to the house. It was about two kilometres away. We arrived back at the house, and he said, "Well, I'll have a drink with you, and I'll take an ounce home with me when I leave."

"Yeah okay, that's fine with me," I said.

I was chilling after drinking my six-pack.

Fizz said, "Help me with this Bourbon."

After a couple of bourbons, we smoked some nice hash cones. I was fucked.

I said, "Well, mate, I'm off to bed."

"Yeah, no worries, I will see you tomorrow, Mick," said Fizz while grabbing his stuff.

I had the best sleep in a long while.

The next day I saw a car for sale and had a look at it. Later that day I bought it. Now I could do runs back and forward to Melbourne to do pickups. So, I started doing that, and for the next year, I was selling a mix of hash and weed, doing stuff to this house such as painting, gardening and renovations. I was drinking a lot though, having nightmares still over the Danny incident. Those nightmares lasted for years later, amongst a lot of other dreams.

A year later, things were getting crazier. There were too many drugs, too much money and too much drinking happening. When you are doing that you get sloppy in what you're doing. When the local cop knows what you're doing, it's not good.

My young cousin Steve came down to stay with me for a couple of weeks. He was a bit green. He never lived a life like mine. He was a mummy's boy who heard stories about me through the family. God knows what, but he looked up to me like some hero. I didn't mind him hanging around. But he wanted to get involved in what I was doing. Trying to copy me I guess, but I knew he wasn't cut out for it.

So, he went over to Fizz's house and was drinking with him. Later that night, they both went out drunk and broke into a couple of houses. During the year there would be a lot of houses vacant because the island was a holiday destination. They decided to break into a couple of unoccupied homes and steal stupid things.

The next morning I turned up to bring Fizz some bags, and they were asleep. I woke them up, and they started telling me what they got up to and showing me the stuff like lawnmowers and paint etc., Nothing really good. I was angry with them. I said to Fizz, "Are you stupid? Do you want to fuck up what we have got going? You should know better." Fizz was my age, around twenty-eight years old; Steve was only eighteen. I walked out of there and went home as I had the shits with them.

A few hours later, there was a knock at the door. It was the local cop. This cop was a reasonable guy. "G' day, Mick, listen," he said with a stern voice, "Do you have a cousin named Steve?"

"Yes, why?" I replied.

"Well, I have him at the station, and he has made a statement about breaking into houses with Fizz. Steve told us that you weren't involved, but you have one of the mowers they stole." He was right, and stupid me, grabbed a mower off them because I didn't have one, why did I do that?

I said, "Yes, but I didn't know they stole it."

As the cop looked at me, he said "I think you knew Mick. Listen, hand it over, and I will forget about you having it because I know about you and Fizz dealing in the pot around town. I don't care about that, as it keeps my paperwork down and there are no dramas because those who normally do are stoned and that suits me." I thought to myself, *'Did I hear what I thought I heard from this cop? Unreal.'*

I said, "Yeah, okay, sorry. I will get you the mower."

As I handed the mower over to him, he said, "Well the C.I.B are coming to interview the two boys. So, I suggest you hide what gear you have and keep things low key for a few days and tell your cousin to leave town. Or else, I will be back here to bust you!"

I said, "Yeah, no problems."

He left, and I soon started stashing the dope I had sitting at home waiting for something to happen.

After a few hours, there was a knock at the door. It was Steve with his head hung down, looking sad with himself. The first thing he said was: "Here Mick; this is my statement do you want to read it? You won't be happy. You will probably want to hit me."

I took the statement and said, "I don't need to read it as I know what you told them, you dickhead, and why would you involve me?" I slapped him in the head and said, "Well get your stuff and fuck off home!"

He started to cry. I was thinking, *'Oh my god, he is just a boy.'* He rang his mum, who is my Aunt Helen, my mum's sister. She turned up to pick him up. As she got out of the car, she started to scream at me saying it was my fault, and that I got him into this.

I was trying to tell her that I had nothing to do with it, but she didn't want to blame her boy. I was the black sheep of the family, so let's blame me. It will spread through the family how I did this. That is why I never had much to do with my family. They didn't want to know me because they always heard terrible stories.

Once he was gone, Fizz turned up, but the good thing about Fizz was that he didn't tell the cops anything and had to go to court. He already had a record, so he knew he was off to jail. Sure enough a few months later, he did. He got six months for being stupid.

Living On An Island

I was left to do the selling and to keep things running. I didn't know many of the buyers, only a handful, so things slowed right down. I had a feeling things were going to change. I always used to get those feelings and nine times out of ten; it would happen.

A night at the bar and I am playing pool, a guy Fizz was selling to owed him money, only about one hundred and fifty dollars for some stuff and since Fizz was inside, I had to collect off a few people he gave credit to and one of those guys walked in. He was a bit of a smart-arse kind of bloke; he knew I was doing this with Fizz. I would ask him about paying what he owed to me as Fizz was locked up.

I went over to him; I was a bit pissed myself. I said, "G'day, bud, you hear what happened to Fizz?" He looked at me with this smart-arsed remark and said, "Well yeah, I did, and it looks like I will have to pay him what I owe when he gets out."

I said, "No, you can pay me!" He got smart and said, "Fuck you!" He pushed my shoulder and then sat down at the bar. He ordered another drink. I saw red and pulled out the knife which I carried with me. I put it straight through his forearm; it went right through and into the bar. He was screaming out "You cunt!" Then I punched him right in the jaw and walked out and started walking home.

As I was walking, my heart was racing. I started to think, *'Shit what's going to happen now. Why do I let people get to me like that? He might go to the cops, but he doesn't seem to be that kind of person. More likely he'd grab some mates and start looking for me. Then I would be fucked. Fuck it; things are going to shit anyway.'*

I arrived home, but I couldn't sleep. So I started packing my stuff up and waited until morning, staying up through the night.

I was smoking weed to keep calm, not knowing if Fizz ever told him where I lived or he might have come to score and waited out the front. He probably would have gone to the hospital first so I might have a while.

Well, I thought, *'I can't go back to the pub, and the cops haven't turned up yet; I thought the pub would have called them.'* My mind was racing. I'm saying to myself, *'Well done Mick you have now fucked things up again.'*

The next morning, I had the car packed, and the house locked up. I was out of there, never to return. I headed back to the city wondering to myself, *'Where the fuck am I to go now? The first thing I thought was to go back to the club and explain what has happened to the boss.*

Great, he's not going to be happy with me.'

When I arrived there, sure enough, he wasn't pleased. But he quickly said, "Well you did do an excellent job on the house. I'm going to sell it now. I will make a good deal, so it's probably a good thing. So where are you going to go now?" I replied, "I don't know." He then said, "Well, I will let you stay here for a few days; you can do some work for me."

What could I say? I had nowhere to go; he made money out of me. I didn't want to do the things he wanted me to do, which was to collect money and help setting up his houses with the hydro. But now he's into this new thing. Selling party pills called ecstasy.

I didn't know much about them, but there's a shit load of money in it. I would tag along with a couple of the younger crew and go to night clubs. The bouncers would take a bag off us and sell them to the young kids dancing. Things were changing on the streets, and I was not into this, maybe it's time to change?

I was still drinking and getting angry for no reason, and I didn't care about shit. I would go into these outbursts and hurt someone or steal a car just for the heck of it. I knew I needed to spend some time alone. I ran into an old school mate of mine, Mark the Dutchman was his name. I liked him; he seemed cool.

I told him about what I had been doing. He never liked my crew and said, "You need to get away from them. Why don't you come to my place and I will give you some work."

I said, "Okay, sounds good; what doing?"

He said, "Well, I am dealing in speed and selling guns, and since I know you know a lot about guns, you can help me." I thought, *'Why not?'*

That night I went back to the club and told the boss, "I am off. I'll see you around, thanks for everything." He looked at me like he didn't give a fuck; he was probably off his face. I was glad not to be under his roof. Too much shit happens there, but somehow, I knew I would be back one day for some reason. The trouble is that when you know these kinds of people is you are never too far from it. It's like cancer.

I went to Mark's place. I felt a lot safer with him. Things were off to a good start. We would stay awake for two to three days on gear and run around selling and playing around. He knew a few girls at massage parlours where they would want gear. He would turn up with a loaded fix for them, run in so they could whack it in their arm, and he would run out with the empty syringe, throw it in a bin and go to the next place to whoever called.

My job was to keep him company and to watch his back. Mark had just bought a house to renovate and asked me if I would help him with it. He lived with his girlfriend, who had a couple of kids from her last boyfriend. Mark had a kid with her, a little boy.

They bought this house for them all to move into, as they needed more room. When it is all done up, he said I could stay in one of the rooms. He had an idea that we should use one of the rooms to grow some hydro in, as he knew I knew my stuff about growing it.

Mark said that he would buy the stuff to set it up, and my job was to do the rest. I thought it sounded like a good idea. When it was time, we would go halves in it. "Sure, great, let's go and buy the lights and chemicals," I said. I knew a guy who had clones which would help.

So, we got stuck into setting this up. It took us about two weeks before it was ready. Some days we would be ripping out a wall or putting in a new kitchen or painting the outside of his house. He was hoping it would be ready for his family to move into within a couple of months. We knew that we should get at least two crops out of the plants. That would help me get on my feet, and it would help Mark with the cost of getting his house finished.

After about three months things were looking good, the plants were budding nicely. It wouldn't be too long before we can pull them out to dry. We were excited. Mark was still doing his thing in selling speed, guns and cars, and he did a bit of everything to make money. We would get so wired on the speed that we would work on the house for hours through the night. We were scattered, sometimes not knowing what we were doing, but it was good.

Living On An Island

One night he told me that we have to go for a drive to the border of South Australia to do a deal picking up a few boxes of silencers. You could buy them in that state. He had seen on the black market, and he would triple his money. I said, "How many are we bringing back?" He said, "A couple of hundred." Mark would have made a few grand on them. So I said, "Sure, I will come for the run. What about the plants?" I asked.

"No worries, my girlfriend will call over and check on them," he said.

"Okay, sweet. When are we leaving?" I asked him.

"Tomorrow morning, and we should get back by midnight," he replied.

The next morning, we headed off to the border. Mark drove a black Holden Statesman that had a V8 motor in it. It was a flash car, and it would get us there in no time at all. It was about seven hours later when we arrived at this farm in the middle of nowhere.

I said, "Do you know these guys well?"

"Yeah," no need to be worried," he said.

He was right. We went into the house, and they treated us well. They gave us a feed, and we also knocked down some drinks. We got wasted, and we were too fucked up to drive back. Mark rang his girl and told her everything was fine, and that we would head back in the morning.

The next day we got up and could hear cows mooing and the sheep and dogs, it was a farm. It was a lovely morning, tranquil. Mark went out to the barn shed with one of these guys to look at the silencers. He came back all smiles and handed over his cash. We loaded up the boot, and we were about to drive away when Marks phone rang. It was his girlfriend; he was talking to her while I was saying goodbye to these two nice farm blokes.

Mark was walking around, talking on the phone, looking pissed off. He got off the phone and said, "Mick, we have got to get back now!" We got into the car and drove off.

Mark yelled, "We have been ripped off!"

I shouted, "What!"

"Yeah our set-up is gone, the lights, plants, everything, even my power tools in the shed."

I thought, '*Fuck who, how?*' Mark was saying, "When I find them, I'll kill the cunts!"

I believed him because in the past, I have been with him when he had shot someone, and he didn't talk shit. Mark could not fight, but he knew how to put fear into people with his mouth and actions, so they are fucked, whoever has done this. I wanted blood, too, as this was my future as well.

On our way back, Mark didn't want to stop; he just drove with anger. We talked about who it could have been as no one knew what we were doing. Six hours later, we were back at the house. His girlfriend was there, and the place was a bit messy.

The room was empty; they didn't leave a thing. Why not just take the plants? Why the lights, the water pump, the chemicals and the tools from his shed? Fucking rats, wait until we find them but who and how, were we going to find out? We were devastated, after all the hard work and expense we had put into the crop.

A couple of days went by, and the neighbour, who was a good friend of Mark's popped his head over the fence and said, "The other day these two guys were hanging around the house knocking on your door, I watched them. One of them lives around the corner. They looked suspicious because you can tell no one lives in your house. If you looked through the lounge window, your house is empty, and you can tell the house is under renovation."

Mark said to his neighbour, "Thanks for that. What does he look like?"

He said, "A young fella about early twenties, jeans, long hair wearing a T-shirt with some band on it." Ah. Now we have a suspect.

We headed around the corner and were watching the houses for someone to come out. It was a long street, so we didn't know which house it was. We sat in the car and waited. We weren't there too long when we see a bloke that fitted the description walk out of his house. Now we know where he lives. Mark said, "We will go there tonight, late."

Later that night, we headed back around. I was hoping Mark wasn't taking a gun with, but it looked like he wasn't. We went up to the front door and knocked.

He came to the door "Yes," he said. Mark just pushed him back; I closed the door behind me. He was yelling "What do you want?"

Mark said to him, "You have stolen my tools and crop you cunt!"

He came back with, "Fuck off; I don't have any idea what you are on about."

"Well sit down, and we will find out," Mark said. Mark turned to me and said, "I will have a look around and see what I can find. You hold this prick in the seat." So, I put my knee into his gut and said, "Just stay still."

Within a minute, Mark came out of the kitchen, holding a pH tester, which was blue and had a mark on it. We knew it was ours. Mark also found a leaf dropped on the floor under the kitchen table. He showed me, and I saw red.

"Right who is the other guy who was with you? Where is he?" I yelled.

"I don't know who you're talking about," he continued saying. "What is this about?"

"We know what you did, and we know you had someone else involved with you, so tell us what we want to know," we said to him.

He stupidly said, "Go fuck yourselves." Well that was it I noticed a pair of hand-held hedge clippers sitting on the coffee table probably from cutting our plants with, I picked them up and said, "Tell us where to find your mate or I will cut your fingers off you fucking thief!"

He still acted like a dickhead, thinking I was bluffing, but I wasn't. I grabbed his hand and put him in a lock. I got one of his fingers and said, "It's your last chance, now tell us!" Mark was looking at me as if to say: you're not are you? And with one snip, I cut his finger off. He was screaming so loud. Mark puts a cushion over his face to block out his scream.

I said to him, "Well, you think I am joking, tell me, or I will cut off the rest of your fingers."

He soon changed his tune. "I'll tell you," he said.

Mark grabbed a towel from the bathroom and wrapped it around his finger and hand.

This guy started telling us his name, his mates' name, and where we can find him. So yes, they did do it. Thank god we had the right person because it would have been terrible if they weren't. Now what? Mark said to him, "Well, you're not going to the cops." Thinking, *'We knew this because why would he go to the cops? As he would have to tell them what he did.'* Mark said, "Well, you're not the leader as your mate has all the gear, so this is what we are going to do."

Mark said, "We are going to drop you off at the hospital out the front. You tell them a story that doesn't involve the cops, while we will go and find your mate and if by any chance, you have given us the wrong address we will be back, and you will lose more than just your finger." He was like, "I am telling you the truth he lives at that address."

We went to the car and off to the hospital, where we dropped him off.

I asked Mark, "What now?" He was so angry I could see that he was planning something. "Well Mick, this is what's going to happen. I'll take you to the house, and you are going to pack up your stuff because I don't want you around after what I am going to do. It's for the best mate that you don't know what it is. There's not going to be anymore growing." He gave me a thousand bucks to help and said if I needed more, he would wire it to me.

"Don't get me wrong; you need to move on because there will probably be some shit going down and I don't want you involved." I was thinking, *"What? But we are in this together. Why? I don't understand."* I was feeling angry. I felt like Mark was dumping me. Later I understood whatever he was going to do. In our world, you don't have witnesses for real bad shit because you might have to get rid of them too.

Mark cared enough for me, not to put me in that situation. I did just what he told me to do; I got back to his house, and I packed my stuff. I left and jumped into my old ford and drove away never to see Mark again.

Twenty years later, I still hadn't seen him, a friendship going back to primary school and high school, over with just like that.

Chapter 21

GYPSIE

Driving along the road, I was thinking, *'I might head up north to mum's place in Queensland.'* I thought it was a great idea. Mum had moved back to Queensland again. Anyway, I was over dealing with druggies and thieves; I was getting sick of it all. I turned up at mum's place; she was living by herself after she had split from Peter and she was happy to see me. I was glad to be there, but after a few weeks, the cops came to visit me.

April's mother knew I was back and decided to call them. I guess to keep me out of the way, who knows, but the cops took me away and locked me up in the watchhouse. It was a Friday, so I had to sit in there until Monday morning to face court over skipping bail with the gun charges. I was looking at five years jail, but I didn't care as I felt like my life was shit. Come Monday; I was given three months for skipping the bail and had to face the other charges at a later date.

For three weeks, I sat in that fucking watchhouse waiting to go to the main jail. Each day the truck would come, and there was never any room. It drove me crazy, locked in a room for three weeks. Each day there was something new, you would get drunks and dickheads of all kinds getting locked up, some were there for a few days.

Gypsie

One guy came in, he was quiet, a bikie-looking kind of bloke with a long goatee and covered in tattoos.

"How's it going?" He said as he sat on the floor.

"Hi, I'm Mick." I introduced myself.

"Yeah, I'm Gypsie," he said.

"How long have you been here? He asked.

I said, "About three weeks."

"Oh my god, Why?" He asked.

"Well, there was no room in the truck when it came through to go to the main jail."

For the next week, we talked about a lot of things: where we were from and told some of our life stories. Other guys would come in, and Gypsie and I watched each other's back.

One night a guy came in spitting at the cops, yelling at them, calling them cunts etc. This guy was a real pain in the ass.

I looked at Gypsie and said, "Great, this prick is going to keep us up all night."

"Like fuck!" Gypsie said.

No sooner was he in our cell; he was pissing us off. He came into my room and sat on my bunk next to me and started being a dick saying, "You know who I am?"

I said, "I don't give a fuck who you are; just get off my bunk!"

At this stage, when you have been locked in a cell for twenty-four hours a day for seven days a week, you can get a bit toey. I said again, "Get the fuck off my bed!" This fuck didn't listen.

So I gave him a nice jab with my elbow and knocked the prick out. I just pushed him off the bed and dragged him out of my room and left him there. Gypsie looked at me and said, "Well done." He liked what I did.

Within minutes we hear the cops are coming down the stairs. I thought, *'Oh no, I'm going to cop it as they can see everything we do.'*

Next thing they opened the cell. "Well Mick, we see you fixed this prick up."

"Yeah, he was giving us the shits," I said. There were only Gypsie and me in the cell.

The cops said, "Well, we will drag this shit out and put him in another cell out of your way. Would you guys like some Kentucky Fried Chicken?"

We looked at each other and said, "Fuck yeah!"

These two cops went over the road and came back with KFC for us and said, "Now behave." We were excited to get a good feed, as we had only been getting sandwiches and I was over them. The cops were happy with what I had done because they were spat on and had to put up with that guy's shit too. It's funny how things work out sometimes.

The next day the truck came, this time there was room to take us, finally. Gypsie and I got onto this truck and were taken off to Wacol Jail. I was glad to get there. We went through the system of getting our clothes and shower, which takes a few hours and we were led to a block and shown our rooms. My room was on the top floor, and Gypsie got a bottom floor.

After I made my bed and got settled, I decided I would go down and wait for dinner. I headed down, and Gypsie was sitting at the head of the table talking with these guys. He knew them. He called me over, "Hey Mick, come sit here mate," he said.

He told the others, "This is a friend of mine, okay."

Gypsie

They replied, "Yeah, sure, Gypsie."

Well, it turned out that he was a president of a club on the outside and these guys were members of this club. Gypsie didn't tell me much the week we were in the watchhouse together; he was playing it cool. He said to me, "You can sit here from now on."

Well, that made me feel a lot safer. He had the whole block under him. *'No one would give me shit, so things were a lot easier.'* I thought. Soon I was getting bored and decided to do some leather-work; which I enjoyed and made myself a tobacco pouch.

Each day I would walk around the oval with the boys, we would walk around and around for about an hour then head in for a shower and feed. Each day was the same. I noticed though; it would be first thing in the morning we would walk around. When we walked around the oval, Gypsie would always pick up a couple of tennis balls that would be on the ground.

I didn't think much of it, but it turned out that during the night, a person he knew on the outside would go to the fence from the railway line, where the screws would not be able to see. They would throw these tennis balls over the fence. Inside the balls would be drugs.

Well, I'll be damned, Gypsie had all bases covered. He ran the block, and no one challenged him. He would roll a joint and we would walk around the yard getting stoned but one day there were no more balls. The screws were watching Gypsie closely. A rat was in the block telling the screws what was going on. This rat was always sitting close to the fishbowl, which is what they call where the screws sat behind a large glass panel.

Well, this rat thought he would be safe if he sat close to the screws all the time. So no one could get him, but that wasn't going to stop Gypsie, he would find a way to get to him.

One day I was coming out of the leather room class, and I saw the rat talking to the screws. I went up behind them. They didn't see me and I could hear them talking. The rat was telling the screws about home brew that Gypsie had set up with a couple of the boys.

This rat was giving them info. Walking past, the rat saw me. I went straight to Gypsie and told him what I had heard. I heard that the screws were going to bust him big time. Gypsie shut down all of his things he had going on for now, until things cooled off.

The next day I was walking on the oval with the boys. Suddenly I hear my name called out. Two screws were standing there across the oval with their finger calling me over. I turned and said to Gypsie, "I wonder what this is about?" I then headed over.

The two screws said, "Come with us." They walked me over to a dorm where they put the trouble makers. I walked into this yard where there was wire all around the roof, and there were wire walls, it was like a huge birdcage.

As they walked me in there, I asked, "What's going on?" They hit me with a baton, and I hit the ground.

One screw said, "You have a big mouth, can't mind your own business." One grabbed my head, the other shoved a fork in my mouth under my tongue where your skin holds your tongue and twisted it until it snapped, kicked me, then they got their dicks out and pissed on me.

It was a really hot Queensland day, and there was no shade. I was on the ground choking with my tongue hanging out of my mouth. One screw grabbed a milk carton and pissed in that and put it by my face and said, "In case you get thirsty, you won't talk for a while now will you?" They both walked away then.

I was lying there in the heat in pain, thinking, *'I might die'* and I didn't care. I probably was there for an hour, but it felt much longer. I looked over and saw a screw sitting there in the shade reading a newspaper, drinking a coke. I was thinking, *'You cunt.'*

Suddenly I heard a lady's voice. I thought I heard things in the heat laying there? I felt like I was cooking. I heard the voice again.

"Open this gate," she said. I looked up; it was a nurse who worked there. She told me, "I'll get you out of here."

She yelled at the screw, "Help me get him up." He helped, and she called for some more nurses to assist. They walked me through to the hospital section of the jail. It felt good to be in the air conditioning and drinking cold water. They were taking good care of me. They called the screws 'bloody bastards.'

The nurse asked me when do I get out. I couldn't speak. She opened my mouth and said, "Oh my god, look at what they have done!" They kept me in there for two days and were good to me. They told me that when I get out, I should report them because too many things like this happened. But no one ever did anything. They couldn't say anything because they would lose their jobs. I thought about it.

They took me back to my block. Gypsie saw me walk in and headed towards me and helped me walk over to a table. He told one of the others to get me a drink. He was like a father caring for his son; he was a good bloke. He said to me after the screws walked me away the other day, he thought about what they might be planning. So, he got word to the nurse to check on me.

    I thought, *'Thank god for Gypsie because I could have died.'* I had to communicate by writing down on paper what I wanted to say because I couldn't talk. I wrote down what they did and why. Gypsie already knew why and guess what? The rat wasn't sitting at the fishbowl; he vanished. It is incredible what you can get in your food in jail to fuck you up; broken glass can do damage inside your guts.

Chapter 21

HEADING SOUTH

A week or so later, I had to go to court again. I got off with the gun charges. Mum got me a good lawyer. By the time I was released, from the jail, mum had moved to Woolloongabba, which is close to the city of Brisbane. She met this guy and moved in with him; he was a plumber.

When I turned up, mum was telling me how she was sick of him, and she had been ripping him off by selling some of his stuff. He didn't realise as his house was full of equipment and shit everywhere. After about two weeks there, mum wanted to leave him and go back to Melbourne; I didn't care. So I said, "Yeah, okay, mum." She told me she had a cheque book of his and knew how to sign his name.

When we left, she was going to the bank to make a withdrawal. Mum was like a black widow with men. Once she didn't have any use for them, she would rip them off and leave them for dead. Heading off, we went to the bank. I waited in the car while she went in. About ten minutes later, she came out with a wad of cash. "Let's go," she said.

We headed down the highway. About five or six hours later, we arrived at a place called Coffs Harbour. Mum said, "This is a nice place." So we stopped and had a bite to eat. Mum then said, "Well, I don't want to go to Melbourne. I wouldn't mind a place somewhere around here, maybe just out of town where it is a little quieter."

I said, "Okay, mum, we will drive a bit and see what there is further down the road."

About twenty-five kilometres south of Coffs Harbour, we came to a little town called Urunga. It was a sleepy town, nice and quiet. Mum loved this place.

"Let's go to the real estate and see if they have any rentals," she said.

We headed to the real estate, and they did have a few available. Mum checked out a house that she liked and she wanted it. She gave them the bond and two months cash for the rent. They didn't ask too many questions.

By the next day, she had the keys to the place, no furniture but she was happy. Mum was good at getting things she needed, and how to get stuff cheap. She went into a church or op shop, put on the tears and a story, and would get what she needed.

Within a week she had the house full of furniture and food, she had everything. I said to her, "Mum, you are settled in now, I might take off next week back to Melbourne and leave you here." I knew she would be alright, but mum was shifty. She didn't want me to leave, so she came up with this plan. Now I look back on it, and I could see what she was doing.

She said to me, "I'm going downtown to get some food for dinner." She had been in the shops for hours. I was wondering where the hell she was. Suddenly I received a phone call. "Hey Mick, I met this nice girl, and she wants you to come down so she can meet you, she smokes pot and has some, I am just having a beer with her."

I was saying, "Mum, I'm hungry. I'll meet her tomorrow."

"No, now, come down just for three minutes."

"Yeah, okay," I said.

I headed down to where they were, and there she was out the front of this woman's place having a beer. She introduced me to her. "This is Trinette, and this is my son Mick."

"Hello," I said as I was checking her out.

"Come in," she said, and we headed into the kitchen. She offered me a cone. She was thin, not very tall and had dark skin. I asked her what country she was from, she said that she was born here, but her mum was an American Indian, I thought, *'Interesting.'*

We headed out the back and sat on a blanket, enjoying the sunshine. After about half an hour, mum said, "Well, I'm going home to start dinner. Mick, you stay here, and I'll call you. You both seem to be getting along." My shifty mum had already told her things about me and found out that she was single; she was doing a bit of match-making. I knew what she was up to, and I didn't mind as I was attracted to her.

Trinette was around twenty-seven years old; I was thirty-two by this time; everything was going smoothly. After thirty minutes or so, I said, "I had better go. I'll catch up with you tomorrow."

She replied, "Well, after your dinner you can come back, have a few cones and chill. I'm not doing anything."

I said, "Yeah, okay, I'll do that."

I knew she must be interested in me and walked home thinking, *'When I go back, I'd take my time and ask her out for the next day and go for a walk along the beach or something.'*

Later on, I went back, and one thing led to another, the next day, I said to mum, "Thanks for that setup," she laughed.

I said, "I like her." I spent a lot of the next few days hanging out with her. After about three weeks, I knew I wasn't going back to Melbourne.

Chapter 22

GETTING TO KNOW TRINETTE

Trinette lived in a rundown spooky house. I said if she liked she could move into our place, mum said she didn't mind, it was probably too soon to ask that, but we were getting on. After another two weeks, she did just that. She moved in, and things were going good. I thought, *'Maybe it's time to settle down as I was thirty-four now and was feeling it was time to change my ways.'*

At least I thought it would be a good idea. However, Trinette wasn't sort of ready; she had a bit of a wild side to her. I noticed she liked to drink a lot and it wasn't until a few years later, that it became a problem.

Within another couple of weeks, mum decided she didn't want to stay there anymore. What Mum was doing, didn't surprise me; she was like a gypsy, always on the move. Probably where I get my unsettledness. So, she packed up, and she hit the road. She headed towards Melbourne. Funny that as she was meant to stay, and I was the one who was meant to go, but it turned out the opposite way.

It wasn't long, maybe a few months and Trinette was pregnant and having my baby. I was excited as I thought, *'I'm ready this time to have a family now.'* Nine months later, she had my son. We named him Jayden. I was there when he was born. I cut his cord, which gave me an instant bond with him. It's hard to explain, but I reckon every bloke should do this and experience the feeling.

After his birth, we both were still getting along, but the drinking was worrying me as her moods would change, and she would get nasty. But I kept thinking; *'Well I have a son, just keep moving forward.'* It was a lovely place to live, but there was no work. I got a job as a part-time chef working at a bowls club which I enjoyed. But I wanted more and decided the only way to get it was to move. I asked Trinette if she would be interested in moving.

She said, "Yeah, but where to?"

"Well since we were in New South Wales we can head north to Queensland, or south to Melbourne," I told her.

She said, "Well, I have lived in Queensland, but I have never been to Melbourne, so let's go there." "Okay," I said.

We planned the trip and packed up and went there. I knew by moving; I had to do things straight and not get involved with my old way of life. We soon arrived in Melbourne and landed at my cousin, Debbie's place. I always got along with her; she was Steve's sister. Debbie let us stay there. She just had a baby girl. So the two women had things in common. I soon got a job driving forklifts at a truck yard. It wasn't long, about two months when we moved into our own house and things were going along well. Trinette was working too, cleaning homes and buildings in the city.

After about twelve months, I bumped into one of my crew members; he asked where I had been and asked me to come down to the club. I wasn't that interested, but not thinking straight, stupid me, asked him to come over to my place for dinner. Everything was going fine. I hadn't had any mates because I focused only on my family.

Looking back, I should have kept it that way, but without realising, you get slowly hooked back in. It started with one old friend and led to another, and another, and before too long you're sucked back into the thick of it again. Sure enough, that's what happened. Before too long, I was seeing this person, that person, back on the drugs and making money on the side, instead of work.

Chapter 23

MAKING IT WORK

I got an offer to take on this house on a property out Werribee way; it was huge. The house was twice the size of a regular place. The hallway was at least a hundred feet long. It had a barroom, the walk-in wardrobe was as big as a bedroom, and it had a garage that could house six cars. It was offered to me by the boss.

Yep, he had plans for me to take on the house for cheap rent, and half of the garage was set up to grow hydro. His cut would be seventy per cent. For security, his cousin Mark would live in the garage. I knew Mark over the years, and we got on well, but he was a heavy drinker. I had two Rottweilers, they were big dogs which I already had, and there was an electric fence around the property, so it was well protected.

We moved into that place and set up the hydro. The first crop I made my thirty per cent, which was around three thousand dollars for ten weeks' work. I was enjoying doing it; I decided to start my own business. So I got flyers made to deliver to all the new houses around my area saying I could lay turf and do landscaping. I knew how to do that, and I decided to give it a go and see how it pans out.

Making It Work

The first week I had three quotes to do. I quickly brought a trailer, shovels, and a wheelbarrow, I was off. I got an ABN number and an account with a turf farm. The business was growing fast. It got that busy that I quit my other job forklift driving and was now doing turf and landscaping full time.

After two years of doing landscaping, I now had three people working for me. I had real-estate agents giving me houses to do. I was proud of how I was going. But as quick as I was raking in cash, it was going up Trinette's nose, and she was drinking more.

Our relationship was deteriorating. I was pushing out the hydro making money there, carrying around two wallets full of cash, I was on a high. There were pool games after work, drinking with my workers, I felt good, and things were going right for me for a change.

One day I received a phone call from a developer asking me if I would be interested in doing twenty-five houses for him, laying turf in the front and back yards. "Shit yeah," I said.

The job was going to make me some terrific cash. Around fifty thousand dollars! So I signed a contract and a few weeks later started to work with these houses. He gave me a five thousand dollars deposit to start on them. My workers were happy with plenty of work; it was going to take around two to three weeks to finish the job.

Meanwhile, out of all the times for this to happen, I received a phone call out of the blue from the adoption agency, saying they had found my brother, Mark. He was in Perth and wanted to talk to me. I nearly fell backwards, after all this time waiting. I never celebrated my birthday as his birthday was on the same day as mine, but he was twelve months younger. I always wondered where in the world he was. It was still something sensitive for me, as though a piece of my heart was gone.

Finally, I was thirty-nine years old, and I heard this news, I was shaking. Later that night, I received a call, and for the first time, I heard my own brother's voice. I didn't know what to say, what do you say? He was crying. He said he had always known he was adopted and wanted to find his mum and dad. Along that journey, he found, he had two siblings as well. All through the years of him growing up, he had his birthdays but had never suffered like me on that day. He asked where I was. I said, "Melbourne."

He then said, "Well, I'll be on the first flight." He was right, the very next day he flew into town. I was at the airport, nervous, excited and shaking, waiting for his plane to land. When I saw him, I was amazed at how much he looked like myself and my cousins. I knew he was the real deal.

Chapter 24

Family

When we got out to the car, I couldn't stop looking at him, his fingers were the same as mine, pulling out my driver's license, I showed him that my birthday was on the same day, same month but a year later, something he didn't know. He was shocked, he pulled out his license and showed it to me and sure enough, was a year later on. He didn't know what to say except sorry he couldn't find me sooner.

When we got back to the house, I showed him his room, and I sat in there with him all night, him showing me his photo album and telling me how he grew up in England. His parents were so wealthy they had maids; he lived a different lifestyle to me. I had no photos to show him as mum had those.

He asked what our mum was like; I said, "That's a long story." I told him a little, but I said you would need to meet her yourself. He couldn't find her, as mum was always using different names and was running from someone.

But he was here, and I was over the moon. I told him what I had been doing and how I grew up. He said, "Well, I left England fifteen years ago and went to Japan, where I taught English, and that's when I got married to a Japanese woman and had a daughter." I was shocked and kept listening as he showed me pictures of his family.

He showed me a photo of these guys in a restaurant. He said it was one of the oldest restaurants in Japan. I said, "Who are those guys with all the tattoos in the kitchen?"

He said, "They are my brothers-in-law."

'Oh, shit,' I thought, *'Are they who I thought they were? Yes, they were Japanese mafia.'*

He told me that he was in thick with them. So much so, that he was doing things that not many westerners would do in that country. Now the plot thickens.

He went on to tell me, "But I fucked up, I left my wife and took off with a younger Japanese woman."

'Oh, shit,' I thought.

He said, "She is in Western Australia waiting for my return; you should come back with me." I said, "I would love to, but I have too much going on here at the moment."

I could see that he thought I wasn't interested in him, but that wasn't the case. I had done a lot in the past two years, and he must respect that. He stayed for about two weeks. In that time, he had seen my hydro set-up and came with me to help lay some turf. But I could tell he hadn't done a hard day's work in his life, his hands were so soft, he only helped me for two days, and he was exhausted.

He stayed back at the house. At night when I got home, I would get told by Trinette what he had been doing. She said, "I am sorry to tell you this, but he is weird. He stays in the bath for hours and walks around the house naked."

I was thinking, *'What?'* She went on to say, "After he ate off a plate, he would smoke a cigarette and stub out his smoke butt out on the dinner plate. He told me, I am no good for you, that I'm just Aussie trash, my brother needed a Japanese woman who would look after him," he said.

After all the time I had never spent with my brother, I didn't need to get angry, but I was upset hearing all of the stories. There was more, my workers were now coming to me saying "Mick, we know he is your brother, but mate, he is asking us for smokes all the time and drinking our beers. He shops and buys himself stuff but doesn't replace our smokes or beers." All I heard now, is he's doing this and that, I was getting sick of it, so I asked him why he was doing it.

He said in his country when a guest comes; they don't pay for anything. I said, "Well sorry mate, you're not in your country now, you're in Australia, and we're not like that, so buy some smokes for the boys." He couldn't understand why I said that, so things were starting to fall apart between us already. I could not believe it, so I suggested for him to see mum as I managed to get hold of her address.

Mum was living in a country town in Victoria, and while he was visiting her, he could see our sister Karen as well, she lived only about a hundred and fifty kilometres from mum. I said to him that to make things easier; I would take a couple of days off work and go with him.

I took time off work. I left one of the boys in charge while we took off for a couple of days. I thought, *'This might be a chance for us all to bond away from the house and my workers.'* We arrived at mum's place, and that didn't go down well, as she didn't want to know anything about it. It was as if she didn't want the past to show its ugly face. I don't know what was going through mum's head, but she didn't want to sit down and talk about anything, and my brother was so upset.

So, we headed to my sister's instead. She was excited to meet him, and when we arrived, it went down well, of course, and out came the grog. Trinette and my sister got pissed, and they were getting louder. I didn't drink as I needed to drive back, besides I wasn't feeling like it. Karen was up all night that talking to her new brother. I was still upset about what had happened during the last few days.

The next morning Karen came to me and said, "Mick, he is strange, he acts like he is Japanese, wandering off, talking their lingo. He even goes to the fridge and drinks the milk straight from the carton, which I hate." She continued to say, "I won't even let the kids do that, and he has smoked all my smokes, he is strange."

I said, "Yeah, I know." Later that day, we headed back. When we were there, he decided to have a bath. I suggested, "Why don't you have a shower?"

His answer was: "We don't shower in Japan, we bath."

I was getting pissed off, thinking, *'Mate, you're not in Japan.'*

While he was having his bath, my son, who was now around five years old came out of my brother's room with this biscuit tin. I said, "Put that back, Jayden."

He said, "Dad, here." So, I took it off him and thought, *'I wonder what he has in this.'* I opened it and 'fuck me' it was full of money, one hundred dollar bills, I reckon over ten thousand dollars. I saw red; he had been bludging off everyone while he had all this. I wasn't happy.

As soon as he got out of the bath, I said, "Listen here, what's all this?"

He said, "Oh, just some cash I put away. It's for us when you come back to Western Australia with me."

Family

I said, "You know what I don't give a fuck about going anywhere with you, so you have until the count of ten to get the fuck out of my house before I use my hands to flog you."

Well, he took off that quickly. He was outside with his stuff. I had time to think of what I had said and thought, *'Don't fuck this up Mick, after all these years.'* I should go outside and say sorry for losing it. I went outside, and he wasn't interested.

He just kept saying: "Leave me alone." So I went back inside, and I never saw him again in my life. That chapter in my life was over. I now know who he is and what he was. I just got on with getting these houses done.

It was my birthday a few weeks later. For the first time in my life, I had a birthday cake and enjoyed myself instead of being sad, I was happy. I got to finish the houses and went to collect my big cheque. The payment was going to take my business to the next level. But more the fool me. I headed into their office to find painters, plasterers and plumbers who were all there to collect their money. Only to find that this guy has done a runner on us. I was so angry, I said, "Can't we find him?"

The others just said, "Good luck, but if you do let us know we want to kill the prick."

Returning home with my head down, thinking, *'Why me?'* Now I owe money to the turf farm, my workers, the soil guy and a few others. *'What the hell am I going to do? Well, I'll have to try and dig my way out of this, but it was going to be hard,'* I thought.

There seemed to be more shootings in the neighbourhood. I heard that there were gang wars over drugs and turf wars. The next generation of crims was now selling ecstasy and a new drug called 'ice.' Ice ends up being the fuel of all the problems. I watched my crew of mates using it and getting paranoid; they were killing each other.

A mate of mine, Benji turned up at my house, and he told me how he'd been hanging out with these guys. It turned out they were the Carlton crew; Carl Williams and names like Mick Gatto, all underbelly crims who were starting to be household names. I didn't know them, but I remembered Mick Gatto from years ago, on the night my uncle took me to the two-up place in North Melbourne. So, I had an idea with whom Benji was hanging around. I met Benji years ago as well, when I was hanging around bikie Steve in Sunshine, he and Benji were selling pot back then.

Benji turned up at my house; he found out where I lived from another mate and thought he would catch up. Not knowing, he was in a little bit of trouble and was in my area as he thought he would lay low for a bit. I said, "What's been going on, Benji?" He was a bit shaken up, I noticed.

He told me he picked up a girl not far from here yesterday and took her down the back beach, at Point Cook, in the Werribee area, and fucked her in the back seat of his car. Benji had a nice black car, I think it was a Holden. After they had spent the night together, he drove her back to the end of her street and said, "See ya later." She asked if she could see him again. He told her to bugger off, that he just wanted sex, so piss off, or something along those lines.

The girl ran home and told her brothers that this guy picked her up and did what he did. So now these brothers were out to get him.

I said, "How do you know they are out to get you?"

He told me he saw them, in their car with her and they chased him, but he got away from them and drove here. I thought, *'Something is not right.'* He stayed overnight, and we spoke about people we knew, and he was telling me about the nightclub scene.

The next day he left, and I got back into work. A few days later, I received a call in the middle of the night, "Mick, can you come to get me?" It was Benji again.

"Yeah, okay, where are you?" I asked.

He said, "I'm at Laverton." Laverton was about ten minutes from here. "Those guys have just run me off the road. They tried running me into a truck, and my car is a total right-off!" "Okay, I'm on my way," I said.

It was ten o'clock at night and cold when I arrived there, I could see the car up ahead, and Benji was standing on the long, dark narrow road. After seeing the state of the car, I pulled up and said, "How the fuck did you survive?" I noticed that every panel on the car was damaged. He told me he spun around and around hitting the fence on the side of the road; the car was a big mess. Benji said, "Those guys are dead!"

I said, "Have you called a tow truck?"

"Yeah, it will be here soon," he replied.

When it turned up and towed the car away, he came back to my place to stay for the night. Meanwhile, I had about four cars; two XE Falcons, a Fairlane and my Ute which I used for work. I owed one of my workers' money for wages. So I gave him the Fairlane; that cleared that debt. I had an XE Ford out the front for sale, only had about eight hundred dollars on it.

Early the next morning I heard a knock on the door, two guys asking about the XE. I'm outside talking about the car, and they seemed interested in it. Benji came wandering out the front door just in his jocks and singlet, but with a gun in his hands saying, "Mick these are the guys that ran me off the road." One of the guys grabbed a piece of four by four timber laying on the ground. Suddenly, my son, who was only around five years old came out of the front door behind Benji.

Things were getting a bit hairy; I yelled at my son to get back inside thinking he was in harm's way.

I yelled out to Benji, "Not here please, Benji, not in front of my family." I looked at these guys and said, "Just fuck off if you want to live."

They didn't seem to be too worried about a gun being pointed at them and said: "We will catch up with you." They hopped back in their car.

Benji was yelling, "Yeah, I'll be looking out for you, cunts, and you will be dead!"

I was so relieved he didn't shoot them, I said, "Come inside, mate."

He just put his gun on the kitchen bench and said, as calm as day, "What's for breakfast?"

I was still in shock and angry then I said, "Benji you can't stay here, mate, they could come back, who knows what could happen."

He was good about it, and he said, "I know, I don't want to bring dramas here to your house," he said respectfully. After breakfast as he was getting ready to leave, I said, "You know what, I'll give you that car that I have for sale, which will get you where you want to go." The car had no registration, but he didn't care. I never saw him again after that.

Chapter 25

Money Trouble

Owing so much money, I started to get calls, *'when are you going to pay us?'* The net was closing in on me. The real estate also owed me money from the jobs I had done. But they only paid at the end of each month. I thought, *'Well I'm going to have to borrow the money. I needed about twenty thousand dollars. But who do I go to ask for that sort of money?'*

The boss of my crew said, "Sure, I'll give it to you at one thousand dollars a week you can repay until you pay back the twenty thousand dollars."

"Shit okay I'll do it, as long as I can pay one thousand dollars a week, I'll be right after the first week. I paid the first payment in the second week. Lucky for me, the next batch of hydro was ready. I didn't make anything out of it. He took my share, which was three thousand dollars, so that gave me another three weeks.

He got twenty thousand dollars out of that batch, not bad for doing nothing. He had these setups going at probably twenty different places. So the money was rolling in for him plus other shit he was doing. Some people have all the luck. So, I had three weeks to think about what to do. I knew I was running out of time; jobs weren't happening because I couldn't get credit as I owed money. I cracked the shits and pulled down the hydro set-up without the boss knowing because I had a feeling, things were going to change in a hurry.

Trinette decided to take off with my son to Queensland as she was shitting herself with what had been going on and thought there was going to be big trouble coming. She didn't want to be around when the shit hit the fan. She thought, *'What if those guys came back?'* And *'How was it going to go down?'* So she left. I wasn't happy about that.

Deciding I didn't want to lose my son; I told her I would meet her up there in a few weeks, she was happy with that. I began selling our possessions to make money and had a garage sale. I sold the two trailers I had full of tools for my business, the furniture and made a couple of thousand out of the sale. I still had to get rid of shit loads of things. I paid another thousand dollars to the boss to keep him at bay and put a thousand dollars away for when I left.

There was no way I was going to be able to repay this money. I knew what would happen; even when your acquaintance with these people goes back to primary school. It doesn't matter when it comes to money, the only thing you get from being part of a crew is, having more time to play with it, more than anyone else. I knew in the end; I would probably end up going on a fishing trip on one of his boats, where you don't come back, so now I had to leave and never be able to return.

So after a week of selling everything, I left the house still with stuff in it probably another thousand dollars' worth. I didn't have the time to hang around. So I took off and drove as long and far as I could through the night, had a nap for a few hours and continued driving.

Money Trouble

I arrived in Queensland where my son and Trinette were, at a place called Hervey Bay. It was about three hundred kilometres north of Brisbane and about a four-hour drive. Trinette had a girlfriend there who put her up. I arrived at the Bay and met her at the beach.

As soon as Jayden saw me, he came running and yelling out my name. I was so glad to see him, but Trinette didn't seem as happy to see me. I was wondering why, maybe while she had been here, she was probably partying a bit and screwing whoever. She said to me, "Well, where are you staying? You won't be able to stay there, so you're going to have to find somewhere to go, and I'm not sure if I want to be with you."

I thought, *'Great, I drove all this way to hear this. Her girlfriend has been in her ear, 'just stay single and party with me' she would be saying.'* She was living with a motorcycle gang member and hanging with that kind of people. I knew what was going on, and I felt helpless. But I wasn't going to leave without a fight. I wanted to see my son, and I wasn't leaving him. I had to think fast.

I rented a motel for the night as I was exhausted from the drive. Looking around the place, I noticed it was so lovely and peaceful, like a paradise with beautiful beaches, a quiet tourist spot. I thought, *'I'd like it here.'*

So the next day I grabbed a newspaper and having my breakfast I looked in the 'rooms to rent' section. I thought, *'This will have to do for now.'* I saw one advert which read, *'room for rent two weeks rent and two weeks bond,'* I rang, and this guy answered, his name was Martin.

I said, "Can I come over and see the room?"

"Yeah, sure," he said.

The room was in a two-story house, one street from the beach. *'Wow,'* I thought. Martin lived there for a few years but had lost his mum; she had lived with him. Now he was on his own with his dog, Bella and needed some extra cash. I said to him, "Listen, mate, I only arrived yesterday."

I continued to tell him what had happened with my son's mother and how she dumped me, and that I was staying at a motel. I need a room as soon as possible. I continued to say to him, "If you are happy, I'll give you the cash for the room." He said, "Sure, you can move in as soon as you like."

That day I did move in, and over the next few days I didn't do much, just got to know Martin. He was a bit of a mummy's boy. He was about ten years older than me, and he migrated from England in the seventies. He had done well but was never married. After a few weeks, I realised why he was still single. He was particular in his ways, and no Aussie woman could handle him. He told me he'd been to Africa, where he found a girl online, he was sending for her. I was okay if that was his thing.

Focussing on getting work and seeing my son, that's all that mattered to me at the moment. I was checking the paper each day for work, I had done a bit of chef work a while back, but I was a bit rusty. A job came up as a second chef at a pub. I applied for it and got it, and things were off to a good start. I got to see Jayden every few days, but she was still the same towards me, enjoying herself, drinking seemed to be her thing, but I still wanted to try and work things out with her. Fucks me why, probably because of having a child together, it always makes it harder to let go.

After a few months, she started to come over a bit more. I noticed she looked a bit tired. Maybe she was getting sick of her party life, or perhaps she was wearing out her welcome with her girlfriend. Either way, she was now talking about us getting a place together again, and sure enough after a few more weeks, we ended up just doing that.

We decided to rent a two-bedroom flat for twelve months. Martin decided to sell his house after his bride arrived. She wanted to move to Brisbane, Martin complied. With the money he got from the house he bought a nice house in Brisbane and had money left over. He wanted to buy an old house in the bay, so he could do it up and sell it down the track to make a few extra dollars. He asked me if I would be interested in moving into the house he buys and help him do it up, and my rent would be a lot cheaper. I told him that I would love to do that.

Within a short time, he had bought a place on a few acres. I moved in there, it needed lots of work I could see. I stayed there for about two years and got a lot of work done on the house. But I wanted to go to Brisbane where I could get better-paying work. I told Martin my plans, and he decided to put the house on the market." We packed up and moved to a nice place in Brisbane, which only lasted about twelve months before our relationship ended.

Jayden came with me, making me a single dad and things were more important to me now. I had to be more responsible and think things through properly to do the best for Jayden. No fucking up or I'd lose my son. I started work and found a house for us two and slowly bought the things we needed.

I enjoyed being a single dad as it brought me closer to Jayden. I take my hat off to all the single parents out there. It's a hard gig, but it's also rewarding. Two years of dating a few women, I just wanted to find someone who cared so that I could look forward to a happy future together. I was not doing anything wrong.

Chapter 26

LIFE GOES ON

It's incredible what kids can do, to make one change their ways. I finally met someone, a lovely lady named Tarina. I have been with her for eight years now. Tarina is a genuinely wonderful person. She keeps me grounded and has helped me so much to maintain a reasonably normal life.

My son was about nine years old when it was just him and I. He is now twenty years old, paying his own house off and doing well, makes me feel so proud. Nothing like me, which I'm happy about, and for that, obviously, I did something right after all.

My life is now at peace. Although, I still have a few demons that visit me in my dreams at night. I guess we all have them. I have a good job now and am buying things for myself with clean money, which makes me feel good about myself.

In the end, I guess I finally fixed my compass. Now I'm always traveling in the right direction and aim to keep my compass pointing that way.

The End

Slang words definition:

Skinheads are a gang of guys who shave there heads like punks.
Blow is a term for having some speed or coke when it is snorted.
Crim: Criminal
Cop: Policeman

Michael Taylor

www.ingramcontent.com/pod-product-compliance
Lightning Source LLC
Chambersburg PA
CBHW071921290426
44110CB00013B/1441